Sleeping with my Shoes On

Reclaim Your Innocence, Reclaim Your Power

L.J. Jackson

DreamSculpt
Sonoma, CA.

Title: Sleeping with My Shoes On
Subtitle: Reclaim Your Innocence, Reclaim Your Power
Author: L.J. Jackson

Published by: DreamSculpt Books an imprint of Waterside Productions
DreamSculpt.com

First Edition, 2016
Published in the United States of America

Disclaimer: This book is not intended as a substitute for professional advice for legal, medical, accounting, financial, business, spiritual, or health-related issues that require a doctor or mental health practitioner or licensed professional to address mental disorders, severe depression, or issues that require medication to be treated.

Nor is this book intended to justify the inappropriate behavior, decisions, or actions of anyone looking to make excuses for spending life in a constant state of victimhood, using past issues and circumstances as a way to manipulate others, or live a life defined by their past.

Printed in the United States of America
ISBN 978-1-945949-31-9 (paperback)
978-1-945949-32-6 (e-book)

Cover and Interior Design by Darlene Swanson • www.van-garde.com

Acknowledgments

I want to acknowledge you, every woman around the world, on every continent, who grew up with an experience of lost innocence that rocked you to the core. This left you with a sense that you needed to keep moving, running, drinking, smoking, and stuffing your feelings and emotions—pretending to be okay—all while masking the pain hiding behind your eyes.

To the millions of women and children who've been silenced, trafficked, enslaved, treated as spoils of war, tortured, raped of your innocence, or robbed of your purity—may we continue to raise awareness to help prevent others from experiencing what you've faced, and may we help you find ways to climb up and out of your pain. Remind the innocent child within you that it's okay to take time out to get help and find ways to reclaim your innocence and reclaim your power!

Dedication

I want to thank my mom, Olivia, for being open, willing, brave, and courageous enough to be the best mother you knew how to be to my siblings and me. And for being open and honest about things you would have done differently ... and for doing everything in your power to love and nurture us now.

I also want to thank my friends and family for supporting me in the work that I do, and to my clients (both past and present), thank you for trusting me with your truth.

To my goddaughter, you gave me hope through the light in your innocent eyes and the love in your heart as you talked to me, played, and reminded me of what it was like to run, have, fun, and be as free as an innocent child.

Jared Rosen, without you this book would have still been locked up inside of me, waiting for the chance and opportunity to be shared with the world, the way it was destined to be.

Special thanks to the firefighters who saved our lives when I was young; if not for you, I would not be here today to tell my story. I'd also like to thank the firefighters around the world: may you continue to do all you can to save lives, and on the days you try but arrive on the scene to find it's too late or there's nothing you could have done—may you find peace and rest in knowing you did your best.

How to Read This Book

This book has been written for those who by outward appearances are doing well, but deep down still need help. When no one is watching, you find yourself unsure how to cope with life, emotions, stress, unhappiness, or disappointment after settling for a life, career, or relationship that's less than you deserve or desire.

Because we can't heal what we don't feel, pretend is not there, or don't take time out to address, there's no time like the present to do just that. As you read, take the time to reflect and gain clarity and insight to redefine moments that have been lying dormant inside, keeping you from living an authentic and fully empowered life.

If, like millions of other women, your innocence was stripped away in childhood, as a teenager, or young adult, after reading *Sleeping with My Shoes On* may you feel inspired to proudly reclaim what's innately yours ... your innocence and your power! May you find comfort in knowing you're not alone, you're not the only one, and you don't have to be ashamed, mask your pain, or settle day after day! You will find yourself able to move forward emotionally, mentally, and physically—one step at a time—while at the same time regaining focus to let go of what no longer serves you.

With all that in mind, I did my best to organize this book in such a way to take you through a step-by-step process that you can use with the unfolding of each chapter as you reclaim your innocence and reclaim your power.

To get the most out of this book, *Sleeping with My Shoes On* is best read beginning to end as you are taken on a journey of introspection, personal growth, help, and healing. You will also have the opportunity to acknowledge your past; recognize its impact on your life, career, and relationships; learn to find power in your personal story; and discover ways to use your pain as fuel to move forward successfully and powerfully.

Before we get started, I'd like to clarify that at first glance at the title, *Sleeping with My Shoes On: Reclaim Your Innocence, Reclaim Your Power,* some have assumed that "reclaiming your innocence" is about nothing more than making up for a lost childhood by playing with toys, coloring books, or jumping rope in our spare time. However, that's just the tip of the iceberg and only begins to scratch the surface. And on that note, "reclaiming your power" isn't about "power" in the traditional sense of having influence, control, and authority, but about having "personal power," which I define as our innate, inner strength to use our "voice and choice" to determine what we will do, think, and be in life.

That said it's also important to note that the situations, circumstances, and challenges shared in this book are common to both men and women. However, I've chosen to draw attention and speak from my perspective as a woman based on an ongoing, worldwide epidemic of women and children, in record numbers, being abused, trafficked, and treated as second-class citizens during a time in history when it would seem this would not be the case.

Let's take our shoes off... and

Reclaim Your Innocence
and Reclaim Your Power!

Contents

Introduction ... xi

Chapter 1: Fires of Life ... 1

Chapter 2: Sacred Space ... 15

Chapter 3: Stripped ... 27

Chapter 4: Looking in the Mirror ... 39

Chapter 5: Picking up the Pieces ... 49

Chapter 6: Reclaim Your Innocence ... 65

Chapter 7: Reclaim Your Power ... 81

Resources ... 97

Glossary ... 101

References ... 109

Programs from L.J. Jackson: ... 111

About the Author ... 113

Introduction

I had gotten good at checking out, ignoring my feelings, and masking my emotional pain by pretending everything was okay. That is, until for the very first time, I took off my mask and got real about everything I had been through. A day that led me on a journey of healing from the inside out.

But I still had one burning unanswered question I needed answered before I could truly move on: **"How could God allow innocent children to be hurt?"**, in order to help me make sense of why things like this (molestation, rape, and abuse) happen to innocent children.

But I couldn't seem to find an answer that made sense, or at least put my mind at ease no matter how hard I tried.

So I gave up and went back to business as usual... sad inside, crying almost every day on my way to work and sometimes in between, unhappy and confused. I stuffed my emotions, put my mask back on and did my best to ignore the emotional pain inside from things that had happened when I was young.

Maybe like me, you've been searching for answers or simply learned to move on despite the tears, anger, frustration, or regret hiding behind your smile.

Whatever the case or regardless of the situation or circumstances that led you to read this book, my hope is that like me, you gain clarity, insight, and understanding of your past as you revisit it in your mind's eye knowing it wasn't your fault, none of it.

You didn't attract it or ask for it. You were an innocent child who had done nothing wrong to deserve ill treatment or harm—plain and simple!

May you find answers to questions and at the very least, find yourself able to put your mind at ease, understanding like I did, it's not creator God who allows innocent children to be harmed, but rather people who make the decision and choice to take advantage of our innocence.

Join me on a journey briefly as I share my story with you to help you reclaim your innocence, reclaim your power. Let go of things that no longer serve you so you can free your mind and live the life of your dreams and desires.

Chapter 1

Fires of Life

"Get up, the house is on fire!" my mom yelled. What? How could I have not smelled the smoke, heard the car explode, or the crackling of the flames?

The carbon monoxide had me in a trance as the thick black smoke filled every corner of the room. It was pitch black as I jumped to my feet and struggled to adjust my eyes, hoping the light switch would come on any second, but it didn't. I was scared to move, knowing there were iron bars on all the windows and doors, once there to protect us, now sealing our fate of being trapped inside with no way out. I stood there frozen until I heard my mom say, "Get in the tub, it's cool, and it'll take a while for the fire to reach us!" I followed the sound of her voice as we all made our way into the bathtub.

There we were: my mom's cousin, his girlfriend, my mom, and me, the four of us standing in the dark in complete silence.

"I guess this is it," I thought. "It's going to hurt, but it won't last forever. Eventually I'll be dead and I won't feel the pain." I tried to wrap my head around the idea of burning to death.

After standing for what seemed like hours, it occurred to me that the small rectangular window was covered with bars and too high for us to escape, but maybe, just maybe, if I yelled for help, someone might hear me and get help for us before it was too late. I jumped out of the tub, stood on my tiptoes, and started hitting the window as hard as I could. As the glass broke, I yelled at the top of my lungs, "Help, help!"

My family jumped out and joined in, "Help, somebody help us!"

I could see a bathroom light on in an apartment window over to the left, but there was no response. It seemed that our cries for help had gone unheard. Then, out of nowhere, a firefighter walked up, pulled the bars off, cleared the glass, and we hoisted each other up one by one.

But it wasn't over ... my disabled brother was still trapped on the other side of the house and the fire had engulfed the front of the house where his bedroom was. We weren't sure he had survived.

I scanned the area as we waited, and it looked like our cousin's girlfriend had gone blind as she stood there with her arms extended with white gauze taped to her eyes. A firefighter grabbed my hand to administer first aid; I looked down and was surprised to discover my nightgown covered in blood. I was bleeding from cuts on my hand and foot.

Then finally ... after waiting for what felt like an eternity, a firefighter surfaced with my brother in his arms.

Staring at the charred remains of my mother's car in anger and disbelief, I began to pace. In my young mind I plotted ways to get revenge on the man we believed had set her car ablaze out of spite. I cried uncontrollably.

The events from that fretful night left me with a sense that I could never rest easy again, not without sleeping with my shoes on.

After the fire, I went to bed fully dressed just in case, convinced and determined not to be caught off guard. I wanted to be ready at a moment's notice if anything happened in the middle of the night.

As you can imagine, there was damage to the house and dark gray, charcoal-like marks covered all the walls. But with nowhere else to go, we continued to live there, with the front of the house boarded up with wood.

We did our best to get back to business as usual. My mom went to work and I went to school, but our clothes still smelled like smoke no matter how many times we washed them. The damage had been done.

In fact, I remember sitting in class one day in school and another student making a comment about it smelling like smoke. Embarrassed and afraid of being made fun of, I sat there and pretended like I had no idea what they were talking about.

Eventually it became clear that no matter how hard we tried to make it work, the house was inhabitable. My mom asked around and, after contacting the American Red Cross, we were able to get a voucher for a new place to live.

Over the years I've shared my story about being trapped in that fire quite often, but I have to admit that in trying to recall as many details as possible to share the full story with you, I find myself welling up with emotion and gratitude. In truth, I must admit that sometimes it seems hard to believe, even for me, but it really happened. In fact, the small, yet permanent scars on my right hand serve as a daily reminder of how close I came to dying and facing my own mortality that night.

It also reminds me of how miraculous it all was. Especially as I think back to how close the cuts I had from the glass came to the main arteries in my hand, which could have caused me to lose my life while trying to save it.

I also remember us finding out that our next-door neighbor thought we were gone, so she told the fire department there was no one inside. The firefighters didn't know we needed help or where to begin to look until I broke the glass!

The "Innocent Child Phenomena"

Thinking back, maybe what helped me take a chance was the fact that I was much younger and hadn't experienced as many, what I call *"Fires of Life"* (i.e., grief, loss, death, suicide, not fitting in, abuse) as they had. So I was willing to take a chance.

Amazing, isn't it? When we're children, we tend to take risks regularly, in our adventures and pursuits. Pulling out pots and pans, playing in the dirt or mud, looking through the cupboards, and venturing away from our parents or guardians during trips to the market or whenever we get the chance.

Oblivious to danger, we explore, model after, and test out everything on our quest to find our place within our family and the world around us. We're blissfully unaware that the mistakes, choices, and decisions we make will shape our life and make a huge, lasting impact—for better or worse.

This unawareness, this blissful state, our desire to explore, and test new things, is a phenomenal time in our lives.

Yes, in the beginning, however short-lived, we experience what I call the "Innocent Child Phenomena," a beautiful time in our lives when we are young and innocent, able to run, have fun, and be free. Our time of innocence is a crucial, sacred, and valuable time to be appreciated and enjoyed.

During this time we are innocent, untainted, wholesome, pure, and virtuous. We also seem to have a hopeful spirit, with a trusting resiliency that allows us to take chances, and have confidence in ourselves and our loved ones' ability to care for us and keep us safe.

As they teach us life skills like: looking both ways before we cross the street, the danger of sticking something into a light switch, and why wandering off can be dangerous.

If we were to break down this innocent time in our lives even further, the dictionary defines "innocence" equivalent to being found harmless, not knowing evil, or being found guilty of any specific crime—"like an innocent child." So in essence, an innocent child is supposed to be shielded from harm because we have done nothing to deserve ill treatment or harm.

Experience of Innocence

In fact, our first experience of innocence starts in the womb, while being carried under our mother's heart for nine months—immersed in her world, inside and outside.

During this time, especially between birth and age twelve, we are in our own world, with a focus on exploring the environment around us, tapping into the world of imagination, and believing that anything is possible. We begin to talk and interact with others, inside and outside of our immediate families (extended family, friends, teachers, counselors, advisors, mentors, coaches).

While learning about personal safety as we develop our traits and characteristics, and soak up the behaviors, habits, and beliefs of our loved ones like a sponge.

Aspects of Innocence

On that note, I think it's important to mention that although innocence is an important and beautiful attribute and aspect of our childhood—as I've come to understand it, study, and witness it professionally—not everyone sees and views this time in our life in that way.

As it turns out, the cultural codes, morals, meaning, and value placed on a child's life determines whether innocence is viewed by others as a sign of weakness, something to value, cherish, ignore, or take advantage of.

That said I'd like to share with you the two well-known aspects or views of innocence that you're probably familiar with. The first one views the innocent child as just one of twelve parts of our ego: the time in our childhood when we're in an optimistic state, have a desire to be happy, accept everyone, and always do the right thing, even to a fault.

The second well-known aspect is known as the "inner child" and focuses on the idea that many adults bring unresolved issues: hurt, pain, shame, or regret from childhood into their adult lives. This results in their "inner child" coming out during times of dire distress, uncertainty, and frustration, causing them to respond or make adult decisions in immature or childish ways such as temper tantrums or violence. They are unable to cope or handle stress in a mature, adult manner. They are adults who act like a child, having grown up chronologically but not cognitively, emotionally, or mentally. And they may even be clueless or callous about their need to do so.

As someone so eloquently put it on social media: "Children in adult bodies, mimicking adult lives."

In short, these two aspects bring to light some very poignant points. They emphasize our innocence, identifying that time in our life as a broken part of us, or a part of our ego to be released and let go of.

However, in this book, my goal is to talk about innocence from a different perspective. I hope to shed light on a phenomenal aspect of our childhood intended to set the tone for us to be resilient, hopeful, determined, and emotionally free later in life. What I've come to realize, and hope you will too, is that innocence in and of itself isn't the problem; the problem is the blatant disrespect of our innocence.

Our childhood is the time when we are young and innocent, however short-lived. It's time to be relished and viewed in a positive light, cherished, and leveraged. I time to help determine what allows us to experience joy, happiness, or just feel good from one day to the next, despite bumps in the road and challenges we face.

Knowing and discovering the *Innocent Child Phenomena* will help you tap into your innocence so you can thrive—and not simply survive—and help you enjoy relationships, situations, and circumstances better, even if just a little bit more than before.

Levels of Innocence

There are different levels of innocence that we experience as we go through life. I want to share them with you because these five levels of innocence affect and impact our lives in several ways: our brain and how it functions, our mindset and how we think, our ability to reason and use logic, and our decision-making process, as we rationalize, communicate, engage, cope, and interact. They impact our lives not only throughout our childhood, but also at every stage and phase of our lives.

The levels of innocence are:

1. Womb Level
2. Child Level
3. Preteen Level

4. Adolescent Level
5. Adult Level

Let's take a closer look at our innocence at each level for a more in-depth appreciation. Not surprisingly, the **Womb Level** (womb to one year) occurs from the time we start to grow and develop in the womb, and lasts until we turn one. This is a time that is both influential and often underestimated by many. During this time we rely on sound and are in tune with our mother's energy, voice, and the noises and sounds around us. As a result, our innocence and experience in the womb lays the foundation for how we feel and shapes our personality. In fact, because of this, studies continue to suggest that parents play music and start reading to children in the womb.

Let me be a bit more specific. When you think back to a time when you met a friend's baby for the first time, did you discover that they seemed to have the emotional attributes already of a "happy baby" (smile/laughter), "sad baby" (sad eyes or tears), or "serious one" (serious look or stoic face), based on their responses to your coos or baby talk? It may have left you thinking, "What a happy baby" or "I didn't mean to make the baby cry" or "Hmm, what's wrong with that baby?"

A few years ago, a friend pointed out a photo of a baby on social media. The baby was sitting in her stroller with a serious look on her face, as if she had been here eighteen years instead of eighteen months. Both her nonverbal body language and facial expression came across as tired and stressed. What I later found out was that during her time in the womb (during her mother's pregnancy) and most of the time since she was born (eighteen months), she had constantly heard her parents argue over their bills, financial problems, stresses of life, and how they were going to make ends meet. This resulted in the baby bearing the emotional burdens unintentionally projected onto her by her parents' inability to cope with their *Fires of Life* in more productive, healthier ways—or at the very least, not around her.

This, of course, is just one example of how our five senses are at work in the womb, ready to kick into high gear after our birth. We rely on what we hear, see, taste, touch, and smell around us to help make sense of our experiences and interactions with our parents or guardians.

The next level of innocence is the **Child Level** (two to nine years), with varying degrees of innocence taking place. But the important thing to be aware of is that, during this time, love and connection, along with learning and following "the rules" or expectations of loved ones is high.

This is largely because during this time we still seek to bond, connect, and grow with the help of our parents or guardians, which serves as a model of what it means to have healthy relationships and "*secure attachments.*" This develops when we know we can rely on them and they are consistently available to nurture us and care for our emotional needs, which we'll talk more about in the following chapter.

Our parents or guardians need to send us a clear message that we are safe and things are okay, letting us know they will guide us and show us the way. It is during this time—our time of innocence, with a lack of awareness of the need to shelter our bodies—that we unknowingly find ourselves at a high risk (1 in 4 chance) of being hurt, harmed, or betrayed by someone we know and trust, which I will talk about in much more detail as we go on.

As it turns out, during the next level, the **Preteen Level** of innocence (ten to twelve years), we extend our trust, automatically assuming we are safe in the hands of authority figures such as teachers, mentors, religious leaders, and others outside our home. We are oblivious to the cultural codes of: our local education systems, churches, community programs/groups, and media outlets, and the power of their influence. Our trust in them is a natural progression and expansion or extension of our connections and ability to engage and interact with others meaningfully.

The next level, the **Teen Level** (thirteen to seventeen), is one of the most intriguingly beautiful yet challenging levels, as we find ourselves in that middle space, the space that lies between no longer being a young child, but also not an adult. We feel and think we are grown and independent, or should not be told what to do. Often we do not understand or realize that our brains are still developing along with our ability to think abstractly. We have to learn to not just take people or things at face value or definitively.

As we go through a natural progression of developing our own individual characteristics and attributes, we pull away from our family, seeking more independence and autonomy. We find ourselves desiring love and connection outside our home, especially at school or at friends' houses. Yet, we are not fully aware of the impact the previous levels' experiences have had on us.

This all plays into the current sense of belonging and feeling of "fitting in," influencing us to go into one of two directions:

1. Engage in positive activities and relationships that enhance oneself, or

2. Engage in negative activities and relationships that hurt us and supersede rational thoughts, and cloud our judgment and decision-making, all for the sake of feeling like we belong.

During the **Teen Level** of innocence, we also grapple with our understanding of our own feelings and emotions, puberty, sexual desires/hormones, and actions. We go about our lives feeling invincible and oftentimes feel the adults in our lives don't quite get us.

We then innocently and often naively go into junior high/middle school or high school convinced that we have everything all figured out. Although in truth we are unaware of the intense peer pressure that teens face, the need for self-acceptance, the need to resist group norms, manipulative mind games, popularity contests, and things like teasing and bullying.

To be an exception to the rule, one must be aware and mature enough to rise above and ignore the negative behavior and actually follow the advice of adults who are mindful of this. Learn to listen to that still small voice inside of you, which can help you stay grounded, even at the risk of being considered "a loner" or "different." But for most of us—or at least 80 percent of us—some days and experiences were better than others, while other memories of that time in our life are frustrating.

In short, whether we got our emotional needs met during our Teen Level, or any level for that matter, is an extremely important determining factor in our overall sense of belonging and well-being as we venture into the **Adult Level** (eighteen years and up) of innocence.

With that in mind, here, as in the other levels, we innocently share a desire to look to authority figures to help us, assuming we can trust them to guide us in the right direction with things like college, financial planning, home buying, paying taxes and raising a family. For the record, those assumptions aren't necessarily a bad thing. In fact, a certain amount of resilience, confidence, and a willingness to believe, hope, and dream of having a "good life" is actually important in the pursuit of the life we desire—rather than one where we are just "working for the weekend," as the saying goes.

Our innocence at this level is not the problem. The problem is whether the people we decided to do business with see our innocence as an opportunity to take advantage of us, appreciate it, or see it as an opportunity to educate and empower us as we collaborate, make deals, sign contracts, and do business with one another. In reality, while we sometimes won't be able to tell until after the fact (i.e., "liar loans" in mortgage industry) we can do our best, as far as it depends on us, by checking to see if the authority figures, family members, friends, and experts in our lives not only claim to share similar morals, values, and mindsets, but also have integrity in doing so.

Tying It All Together

The mental and emotional scars are often harder to face. Millions of women and men, sometimes with obvious scars and often not, go on to develop habits of giving up easily, quitting, shutting down, and spending years on an emotional roller coaster ride in response to the *Fires of Life*. You know those traumatic experiences, disappointments, and setbacks that leave us with a need to be guarded, overly cautious, or controlling. After experiencing things like betrayal, heartache, or abuse, which cause us to fear the unknown, feel trapped, protective, and defensive.

Looking back, what I appreciate most about the *Fires of Life* and in my case the real fire, is that it served as a catalyst or vehicle for the work I do as a counselor, mentor, consultant, and certified life coach. I am truly and genuinely passionate about helping others climb up and out of the situations, circumstances, and beliefs that leave them trapped in their past or in fear, worry, or doubt.

Additionally, my experience of being trapped in the fire also serves as a continuous metaphor, symbol, and reminder for both myself and my clients to keep going and not give up on ourselves or our dreams. On the days when we feel engulfed by the flames, overwhelmed, and surrounded, remember that the *Fires of Life* happen to us all (although not in the same way). So even in our darkest hour, when all hope seems lost and it seems like there's no way out, help is available once we're ready to do what it takes to get it.

Now it's your turn to dare to remember a time in your childhood when you experienced the *Innocent Child Phenomena,* a time when you were young and innocent, able to run, have fun, and be free. A time when you experienced being innocent with a childlike wonder, at a time in society when playing outside was the norm and playing make-believe or "pretend" was an adventure. This was a time in your life intended to be beautiful, memorable, and something to be proud of.

As you think back to what you experienced on your journey through the five levels of innocence, just know that whatever circumstances or situations you've faced—be it innocent victim, innocent bystander, or innocent home buyer—the key word was that you were innocent, so you didn't deserve ill treatment or harm.

This means that you and your loved ones now have the awareness to navigate, recognize, and identify the times when education and common sense can make all the difference. At the same time, we understand that we can't control, predict, guarantee, or prevent certain things, no matter how hard we try. This is why there's a need to give oneself the space to grow and develop professionally, personally, socially, and emotionally. As you decide to not allow fear, worry, or doubt to cover up your innocence, leaving you too afraid to make a move, suffering in silence, thinking there's no other way out.

Like me during the night of the fire, sometimes you just have to stand in the silence and start by searching from within.

After coming to understand the five levels of innocence, you can choose to decide to see innocence as a gift of resilience, flexibility, and confidence in life. Despite the carbon-monoxide-like hearts or intentions of those who've shown up and tested your patience and resilience, your job now is to do your best to make sure those you do business with, surround yourself with, or are intimate with have integrity.

Chapter 2

Sacred Space

He looked me dead in the eye and then whistled as we drove by. "Why was he just standing there on the corner? On Thanksgiving of all nights", I thought to myself. Oh well. My mom turned into the driveway and I stood on the porch, waiting for her to turn the key, but something was different.

She opened the door and I couldn't believe my eyes! The house was empty, like when we first moved in. "Wait, am I dreaming?" They had ransacked the place and taken everything! Like a scene out of a movie, our mattresses were turned over, our dresser drawers were piled on the floor, and the place was a mess—like they were looking for something hidden, but weren't sure where to find it.

I went to my room to check. My Nintendo video game, my clothes, and even my shoes were gone. Who would want someone else's used shoes? As a teenager, I couldn't understand why they would stoop so low as to take my shoes, too.

With an eerie view into the night, the door leading from my bedroom to the backyard was left wide open. Had they just left moments before we pulled up? I couldn't believe it, and then I realized that the guy I saw standing on the corner earlier must have been their "look out." He had watched, lurked, and waited for an opportune time to help them come in and take our stuff, on Thanksgiving Day of all days.

They had learned our routine and combed through every inch of the house, but that was our stuff and all we had! And to make matters worse, it was the second time they had ripped us off and taken what my mother had worked so hard for.

I was angry. But as a teenage girl I felt vulnerable more than anything, and embarrassed after realizing that whoever had done this had gone through my underwear drawer and had seen my unmentionables. You know the ones you hope no one will ever see for as long as you live because they aren't as nice as they once were, thanks to "that time of the month."

With my personal space invaded and our possessions violated, I no longer felt like I had a safe space to call my own. Was it our neighbors who lived in the back house, on the side, or someone else? And who would be so bold, selfish, and greedy enough to take shoes from a kid?

With my questions unanswered, my anger turned to rage.

Tired and feeling powerless, I screamed, yelled, and pounded on the bathroom mirror, hitting it as hard as I could until it shattered into pieces. My mom came in and held me tight as I cried.

Angry, frustrated, and fed up, she went out on the front porch, and with weapon in hand, said, "The next #$@&% who comes in our house won't be coming out!" She called the police, filed a report, and thankfully that was the end of that.*

Innocence of Possessions

As you may have guessed, I was left feeling like the house we moved to was unsafe and nothing more than a place of terror and uncertainty. After innocently leaving to spend time with family, we came home to a violation of our property, our space, and privacy. Now even more confused about life, the way the world worked, and wondering if it was possible to trust others and ever have a sacred space or safe haven again, I did my best to move on.

As an innocent child, until we experience moments like this we have faith in others, hope for the future, our dreams and goals, with a list of things to do and achieve as we wake up and get dressed each day. We ask tons of questions of our parents or guardians and spend our days focused on playing, creating, and exploring. And although it may have been slightly different for you, in general during our teen years, we still engage in play, creativity, and exploration, but it just looks different. It manifests itself in sports, hanging out with friends, and playing a different set of games (often riskier) than the ones we played when we were little.

How Protected Are We?

Like my mom after our house got burglarized, parents or guardians can do everything in their power to try to protect our innocence and keep us safe, yet despite their efforts, someone else comes along and takes it away.

This begs the question: after the cutting of our umbilical cord, how safe can our parents or guardians really keep us, or how long will it be before a part of our innocence is prematurely lost?

On the other hand, what happens when parents or guardians themselves don't make an effort to resolve their own trauma and drama?

This question is answered in one of my favorite books, Daniel Siegel's Parenting from the Inside Out (2003), which echoes what I've seen take place over the years after working with hundreds of families as a child development specialist and consultant. It is the belief that the behaviors and attitudes of parents or guardians are mirrored and played out in the lives of their children. This is based on parents creating one of the following relationships and connections with their child, either intentionally or unintentionally:

1. "Secure attachment"—parents who are nurturing, emotionally available, present, and responsive
2. "Insecure or avoidant attachment"—parents who are emotionally unavailable, emotionally or physically absent, unresponsive, and rejecting (i.e., post-partum, depressed, self-focused)
3. "Insecure, anxious, ambivalent attachment"—parents who send mixed signals and messages as they inconsistently communicate or become intrusive vs. protective
4. "Insecure, disorganized/traumatic attachment"—parents flying off the handle, creating fear, chaos or inconsistency due to things like drug and alcohol abuse and mental illness

All forms of insecure type attachments result in a loss of innocence in the sacred space of our brain and our mind, which plays a huge role in how we go on to interact and experience life and others.

The good news is Daniel Siegel (Parenting from the Inside Out, 2003) talks about how, regardless of what kind of attachment we received from our parents, we can go on to create what's called "Earned Attachments" by reflecting back, gaining clarity and understanding as to which type we grew up with. Then we can decide to move forward and create new, healthier attachments and connections for ourselves. I've done my best to share here some key and crucial stories and topics to help you do just that.

Perfect World vs. Reality

Despite the efforts of many, we still have not figured out a way to make sure children are completely protected from horror and terror so they can be carefree and have innocent fun.

In fact, history books, parenting blogs, articles, and social media sites are filled with stories of parents' efforts to keep them safe backfiring, with parents being seen as overprotective, "helicopter" parents, or smothering leaving children often feeling disconnected, smothered, rebellious, resentful, or vulnerable and overly naïve after being too sheltered.

This has subsequently led to millions of gruesome accounts of child abuse, child pornography, trafficking, school dropouts, child labor violations, and children plagued with poverty-stricken diseases and illnesses as they escape with their families as refugees worldwide.

In fact, according to research by the Forgotten Children Inc. non-profit organization, there are more than 27.9 million victims of human trafficking worldwide. With predators, targeting minors who lack supervision, have family problems, insecurities, issues at school, are isolated, or ostracized with a deep desire for love and acceptance.

In a perfect world, we would be able to prevent not only trafficking, but also malnutrition, and childhood illnesses with things like plant-based, nutrient-rich meals, and homegrown or farm-raised food. This would drastically reduce the amount of traumatic losses of innocence, by making a worldwide, concerted effort to have children in this generation and beyond only experience the natural progression of a loss of innocence that fades away over time in a positive way. This would be similar to the rites of passage such as christenings, quinceañeras and sweet-sixteen parties.

However, in reality today's technological advancements such as the Internet and smartphones, are both a blessing and a curse, with it easier than ever for child predators to abduct children by luring them into trafficking circles or selling them by way of online chat rooms, phone apps., and illegal websites. As a result, child trafficking is also on the rise, with more websites than ever luring children as young as 9 yrs. old into life-destroying, treacherous acts. This makes the loss of innocence abrupt, catching us off guard or by surprise more now than ever before.

In spite of safeguards like "parental control" blocking access to channels or sites that require a person be eighteen years or older, still with a click of a button or mistyping of a word, a loss of innocence can take place in seconds after viewing a graphic photo, video, inappropriate site, or movie intended for adult eyes only.

And just like that, like the cutting of our umbilical cord, what's done is done, and we can't go back inside to take shelter in the womb. Instead, like babies, we are out of the safe haven of our mother's womb, and find ourselves with a new point of view, perspective, or outlook on life after our sacred space is gone or no longer sacred.

How This Impacts Us

We come out of the womb and into a family, education system, and society with our childhood shaped by the emotional sanity, safety, attachments, and security—or lack thereof—provided by our parents, guardians, and other adults around us. We are clueless and unaware of any potential risk of harm or hidden dangers, of things like crime, bullies, or unhealthy relationships inside or outside of our family.

We have no idea that the hearts of those around us may be dark, jaded, or tainted, leaving us in harm's way before our life ever begins. This results in us being negatively affected and exposed to danger, witnessing or experiencing traumatic events or betrayal, often leaving us with psychological, emotional, and maybe even physical scars.

This causes us to assign negative or irrational thoughts to our experiences, which in turn leads to a cycle of negative internal dialogue. Our "inner critic" teams up with our unconscious mind to pull from memories and moments that share a history of negativity, replaying them like a broken recording set on repeat.

This increases the likelihood of us making what's happened more about us, and less about the person or people who chose to prey on our innocence and vulnerability. And what's more, our criminal justice system, some outdated laws, societal norms, and misguided philosophies, like the Law of Attraction (which I love, by the way), vicariously perpetuate the belief and mindset that a completely innocent victim, especially a victim over the age of twelve, must have worn, been thinking, or doing something to cause what happened to them.

Truth be told, it's no wonder that many women and children, after having the sacred space of their mind, body, or soul invaded, internalize their trauma as being their fault, blame themselves, see it as a sign that they're not enough, something's wrong with them, or find themselves re-victimized at the hands of others who judge what they don't understand. They forget that being innocent means you didn't do anything to deserve the ill treatment or harm you faced.

Needless to say, as a result this often leads to a ripple effect of self-doubt, guilt, and shame; a need to prove ourselves; looking to others for reassurance, validation, recognition, or attention; and with a hesitance to get professional help and support to discuss our issues, irrational thoughts, and false beliefs. Notwithstanding, of course, those who've attempted to get help at one time or another, and found themselves either uncommitted to the process or feeling mismatched or a lack of connection with the professional expert they signed up with. We believe we have to mask our pain and appear strong, be tough, and move on.

Talking about how this affects us with someone we can trust with our deeper feelings raises our awareness and is highly beneficial. Opening up helps us brings clarity and reduces the likelihood of us beating ourselves up, feeling like we're alone, or feeling the need to build walls—rather than boundaries to protect our sacred space mentally, emotionally, and physically.

How We Deal with This

Studies on childhood, abuse, and trauma in recent years show there once was a time in our lives and in society when innocence was kept sacred or sheltered to a certain degree. Over the course of the last couple of decades, thanks to the Internet, at the push of a button children can watch videos, war, and pornography, and become morally impaired in a matter of minutes, if not seconds. This comes along with even more exposure and the potential for cyberbullying.

On the flip side of the coin, there is also a decreasing right to privacy, our privacy being stripped away in the name of reducing things like terrorist attacks, allowing government entities to tap our phones and track our Internet usage.

Sadly, what may be worse is that children and young adults have now grown accustomed to and are aware of the fact that they can innocently go out and be hurt, shot, or killed. This can happen at places that once posed minimal risk of harm, like nightclubs, shopping malls, or movie theaters. Additionally, young adults who may have managed to avoid experiencing a loss of innocence in childhood, often as young adults (eighteen or older) in college or while starting a new career find themselves facing a loss of innocence through things like date rape on spring break or at parties, violence in the workplace, civil unrest, tuition hikes, or discrimination.

With all that, one thing I want to stress is that what's needed is not a quest for "the good old days," but rather reliable, timeless tips combined with modern-day tools and safeguards. These include a blend of new forms of action, self-protection, precautions, and awareness to help, heal, and strengthen things as a society when it comes to education, housing, and finance. Equally, we need to change the sexually laced images placed in ads, commercials, and shows and strengthen the societal messaging through the media for the well-being of children.

Safety Plan

In spite of the challenges, we can do our best and be proactive in educating innocent children in both our immediate and extended families by having difficult, yet informative and sometimes honest and candid conversations about the world and the precautions they need to take.

In addition, we need an increase of educational/life skills/ safety videos, and books as well as visits to the local police department and increased community engagement and memorization of emergency locations and phone numbers. We need more education for self-development and self-defense, like Karate and Tai Kwan Do classes for kids. It is essential that they know how to defend themselves and protect themselves from "stranger danger" on their way home from school, as well as undercover predators who lie dormant like termites in your home or community. Not so that they live in a fear-based emotional state, but rather to empower them and protect them morally and sexually.

After a loss of innocence, this is even more of a challenge. We create self-fulfilling prophecies and a bad habit or inviting in unhealthy or unsafe people. We can swing from one end of the pendulum to the other, either having no filter or boundaries about those we let in, or by letting no one close at all.

Moreover, as adults putting ourselves out there and letting others in, there is a delicate balance and need to set up boundaries, learn who to trust, who's safe, and who could be toxic to us and should be avoided. Most people at one point or another in their lives may have an issue with friends and family showing up and taking more than they give in a relationship.

As you think about your life, what type of safety plan do you need to improve or put in place? Is it a plan to keep your positive mindset from being stolen by negative people around you? Do you need to create better boundaries to make sure you and your children aren't walked over or taken advantage of financially or emotionally? Or does your safety plan need to include seeking help from experts who can help you also create an "exit strategy/ exit plan" to leave an abusive relationship safely.

Maybe for you it's just discovering how to communicate more effectively and safely, so as to not cause harm and damage to the ones you love the most. For others, it's spending time creating healthy connections, moving to a safer neighborhood, or taking self-defense classes. Whatever the case, remember you've got nothing to prove to anyone, and your only job is to protect and take care of you—with the hope, resources, and support available to help you get started.

Tying It All Together

Despite all the challenges and pain I faced while growing up, I must admit that I did have moments of normalcy in my childhood. I skated, rode my bike, played hopscotch, participated in spelling bees, hula-hooped, played double dutch, and tetherball on the playground.

But for me, having our home burglarized and knowing someone was watching us and willingly came into our sacred space left me feeling vulnerable, terrorized, and unsure if I could ever feel safe again. I learned the hard way that my surroundings and connections weren't as healthy or secure as they once seemed.

Some of my friends think I have too many boundaries and am overly cautious nowadays, and quite honestly they are probably right. But what I'm sharing with you in this book is only a small part of what I've witnessed, seen, heard, and experienced. So these days I'd rather err on the side of caution than live with the regret of knowing I ignored my instincts just to appease others.

I also must confess that I've attended safety and self-defense training over the years, and while I'm no expert on self-defense, the top precautions shared are typically:

- Beware of your surroundings
- Walk with purpose and your head held up high so your body language sends a message that you're not vulnerable and weak (and that you will fight back)
- Follow your instincts
- Have your keys ready so you don't have to fidget or fumble to find them when you're walking to your car or house.

I understand that there's a thin line between cautious and paranoid, so I make a concerted effort to not allow my past to dictate my present, keeping me locked in a bubble, too afraid to live, interact with others, or go outside and get rays of sunshine and Vitamin D.

I also know that my male friends and family members don't have to deal with the risk of things like being raped, kidnapped, or trafficked on the same level as we do. For that reason, creating a safety plan is a must, and not an option in my opinion. It can be a safety plan to guard your heart, your emotions, or your mind, body, and soul. Remember, as the saying goes, "Our body is our temple," our sacred space, and regardless of what's happened to it in the past, it's our job to do what we can to protect it mentally, emotionally, and physically as far as it depends on us.

Chapter 3

Stripped

I turned to walk away and there he was, apologizing for hurting me, saying he missed me, he just wanted to talk, and be friends. I was fifteen and he was nineteen.

The last time he had said that I knew what would happen, so I attempted to spray him with an old can of mace, but the stream fizzled down, got all over my hands, and in my eyes, making it easy for him to rape me. That's why this time I was determined—things would be different.

I found a green glass bottle in the dirt outside near the door, picked it up, broke it, and waved it at him to show him I meant business. But our scuffle ended quickly, with him knocking the bottle out of my hand, pulling me inside, and throwing me to the floor.

It all happened so quickly. As he held me down I drifted away, pretending like it wasn't happening as he taunted me and said things like, "You're ugly, nobody wants you, you ***b$@&%!*** *I don't know why I bother!" He left.*

Embarrassed and ashamed, I soaked in the tub and did my best to scrub him away. But I could still hear his words playing in my head over and over like a recording, and as I stood in front of the mirror brushing my teeth and combing my hair, all I could think about and hear was, "You're ugly, and no one wants you."

His lies became my truth and from that point on I criticized every inch of my face, noticed every pimple and blemish, and avoided mirrors, looking down or running by them at places like the mall so I wouldn't have to look at myself at all.

The more I listened to my "inner critic" mimicking those dreadful words loud and clear, the more my thoughts became irrational as I racked my brain for evidence to confirm that he was right. After all, if he wasn't, then how could I explain why I hadn't found love (not realizing that I was only a teenager); unless it was true that no one wanted me? I then applied those same irrational thoughts to my relationship with my dad and I asked myself, "If my dad really loved me, then why did he leave me too, when the relationship ended between him and my mom?

Unfortunately, by the time I met my abuser, I had already lost confidence in my loved ones' ability to care for me, and I didn't know what healthy boundaries were or how to recognize healthy love. Consequently, I dated and messed around with any guy who paid me some attention, unintentionally created my own self-fulfilling prophecy of being unloved and unwanted. I dangerously dangled on the slippery slope between logic and reasoning, with my thoughts seemingly making sense, though often not correct.

I wish I could say that was the first time I was physically violated, but in actuality my sexual purity was stripped away when I was only eight years of age, while my family was away, and again when I was eleven, as the adults partied in the other room. Then sadly at thirteen, after I innocently said my friend's uncle was cute and I wanted to know if he was around our age, before he called me into his apartment and closed the door. Confused by his electrifying touch, I didn't really quite understand how to make sense of it all; especially after learning he was twenty-one with two-year-old twin girls of his own.

As you may have guessed, by the time I turned sixteen my sexual morality was impaired, my gauge for boundaries was almost nonexistent, and my understanding of healthy connections and safe people was definitely warped more and more with each interaction, violation, and experience.

My innocence had been stripped away, with loss taking place at every level.

The Loss of Innocence

The loss of innocence can take place at the hands of a complete stranger, between you and another child, or by way of a friend, a friend of the family, or family member.

During our formative years, some of the most common experiences of lost innocence stem from things like bullying, shunning, sexual perversion, sexual harassment, sexism, rape, racial conflict, moral perversion, outbreaks of violence, and property damage.

Maybe, like me, you experienced a physical loss of your possessions or sexual purity; or perhaps your loss was less about you, and more about what you heard or saw.

As a school counselor working with hundreds of students every year, I wouldn't say I've heard it all, but I have definitely heard a lot. However, it never gets any easier when students come to me and say they've been abused or raped. After ten years it still breaks my heart, especially when I contact the necessary authorities and the student's claim goes unfounded because it couldn't be proven or their wasn't enough evidence to do anything about it, or they're asked why they waited so long to say something about it.

In those moments I witness the light in their eyes get a bit dimmer, or flicker and then go out.

That is often the emotional response after any experience of loss, even if just temporarily: feeling tired, drained, misunderstood, unheard, or powerless and without a voice. As we make what happened about us, rather than the person who carried out inappropriate actions: and their own unresolved issues, egos, mindset, and choice to take advantage of our innocence.

Unfortunately this leaves us feeling ashamed, angry, and frustrated, asking ourselves questions like, "Why did that happen to me?", "Why did I trust him?," "Why doesn't anyone believe me?," or "Why did I go to that event or party?" Often we don't realize—like the personal development expert Anthony Robbins often says—these are "disempowering questions," questions that lead to answers that make us feel insecure, sad, or powerless.

We need to develop the ability to ask "empowering questions," questions that lead to answers that make us feel confident, accepted, forgiven, powerful, and loved. Then we are able to move on sooner, with our heads held high, knowing it was not our fault, we were innocent, and we are not to blame. Some empowering questions are:

- "What happened in their childhood that makes them act this way?"
- "What kind of healthy boundaries do I want to create for myself after what happened?"
- "How can I use my pain as fuel to reignite, keep going, or get back what was lost?"
- "What do I need to give myself permission to feel now?"

- "What types of support do I need now: an ear to listen, a journal to write, professional help, time to feel, deal, and heal?"

So we don't build walls to guard our hearts and develop a habit of searching outside ourselves for someone to come along and fix it, rescue us, or confirm our worth and validate our existence.

Child Maltreatment

Initially, I thought and assumed my experiences were rare and for whatever reason there was something about me that made me an easy target or easy prey. So to fix it I thought I needed to figure out how to make myself less desirable. Sadly, an all too often common story and one of the top reasons many women in weight loss programs confess to overeating, overindulging, being obsessive, or controlling, to attempt to try to fix, bury, or cover up what they've held on to from childhood.

It wasn't until later in life that I discovered that even today, molestation is common. For most girls it is often a generational cycle of abuse with a chain that someone needs to break to keep it from continuing.

In fact, I later learned that a lot of the women in my family lost their innocence by being raped or molested when they were girls, either by a family member or a family friend. But no one knew or talked about it growing up.

I was even more amazed when I attended an event on the subject and found out that child maltreatment affects and impacts women all over the world. And that issues of child maltreatment are often compounded during our K-12 experience, since we spend such a significant amount of time in school subjected to often demoralizing labels such as fat, tall, short, slut, "easy", stupid, or dumb. These kind of labels bring about judgment, bruised egos, a need to live up to labels, stereotypes, self-fulfilling prophecies, and so on.

To break it down a bit more, this also shows that we start in a state of innocence, assuming that positive life experiences, healthy connections, and interactions are automatic. But the reality is that the average person experiences negative life experiences—traumatic, shocking, unhealthy connections and interactions—more often than one might think... in the two places they spend their most time: home and school.

I recently took a look at the World Health Organization's study on child maltreatment. They define child maltreatment as abuse and neglect that occurs to children under eighteen years of age and includes all types of physical and/or emotional ill treatment, sexual abuse, neglect, negligence, and commercial or other exploitation, which result in real or potential harm to the child's health, survival, development or dignity when it comes to a responsible relationship, trust, or power. Another form of child maltreatment is exposure to intimate partner/domestic violence. The findings show that a quarter of all adults have reported being physically abused as children. That's one out of every five women and one in thirteen men who report that they have been sexually abused as a child.

If it's happened to you, you're not alone and you're not the only one. Child maltreatment is a global problem that causes serious, life-long consequences, with a likelihood of effecting 80 to 85 percent of children. This creates a negative ripple effect in their lives and inhibits their social life and careers, which confirms what I've seen recently from over two hundred adults looking for life coaching, career coaching, organizational/time management coaching, health coaching, and/or some type of counseling or therapy.

Child Labor

While there have been attempts to protect children and keep them from being taken advantage of since the creation of child labor laws, police stings and raids, organizations like UNICEF, the Forgotten Child, Inc., as well as groups like Human's Right's Watch continue to find that children are still being forced to work in fields, factories, farms, and mines. Children are forced to become day laborers, shoemakers, cocoa bean/tobacco/farm pickers, and miners with companies and organizations profiting most from vulnerable, poverty-stricken families.

Along with that, there have also been stories of children being promised things like athletic scholarships in other countries in exchange for their family's livestock/goods. However, more often than not, they discover it was a scam, their possessions have been taken, and their children abandoned in a foreign country. Leaving them and their children shocked, stunned, after being left to fend for themselves far away from home.

My heart and intention in sharing these facts with you is not to overwhelm you or make things seem bleak when it comes to children, but rather to cultivate an awareness of how vulnerable and susceptible we are at that age. As a reminder a large portion of what happens to us early on in life is shaped by our family and the world around us, has the biggest impact on our future well-being.

That being said, the good thing is that as children we are resilient and with help, support, and opportunity we can rise above whatever we face the first eighteen years of our lives.

Let me explain what I mean. At the very least, knowing this, talking about it, and becoming more vigilant, proactive, and aware, gives you and those around you the opportunity to be empowered simply by knowing more than you once did before and possibly keep it from continuing locally, nationally, and potentially globally. Also, shedding light and providing insight about the difference between "disempowering" questions versus "empowering" questions can help make a difference.

Adult-Child Experiences

I'd like to share one last thought about what happens with the premature stripping of our innocence.

Simply put, it's the "adult-child" experience, an experience that usually occurs unintentionally after families create an environment like I mentioned earlier, where there is little to no time, attention, or effort made to ensure a child's emotional attachments and connections are secure. So they can experience healthy, guilt-free communication and have time to just be a kid and focus on kid stuff and their education.

To be clear, the "adult-child" experience is not the same as having to do chores around the house or show some responsibility by helping out during our formative years.

On the contrary, as you can see from the issues of child labor, the "adult-child" experience is one in which children are required to grow up quickly, and engage in activities intended for adults. Children should not have to experience or worry about issues such as paying the bills, keeping the lights on, participating in forced child labor to feed the family, and raising their siblings.

In other words, when this happens the child takes on an adult role, and often experiences a role reversal, with them taking care of their parents instead of the other way around. This keeps them from being able to run, have fun, and be free.

On a larger scale, this leads to the potential for millions of children to find themselves socially awkward or out-of-place as teens, quietly withdrawn, apathetic, disconnected, or avoiding connections, as they start to believe that others can't be counted on, trusted, or relied upon.

For the communities I work with, our research shows that about a third of families are simply unaware that putting their children in such circumstances and situations are causing stress, strain, and a ripple effect of negative actions and behaviors. Other members of the community want their children to succeed and do better than they did in life. So much so that they are unintentionally forcing their children to grow up quickly and participate in tons of extra-curricular activities and advanced classes so they'll be competitive in the job market or life. But unfortunately, there is also the bottom tier of our families that are on survival mode or simply don't care.

In more recent years, I've personally seen the "adult-child experience" become more and more common in the county I work in, due to things like homelessness, teen pregnancy, and children with parents or guardians who work graveyard shifts or aren't earning enough income to pay for the family's necessities.

This begs the question: Can anything be done to decrease the rise of children having the "adult-child" experience and if so what?

Yes. Most parents and guardians do care, although it may not seem that way, and what we found was that something as simple as parenting classes, community support, resources, and tools to turn things around is needed most. Something, important to understand as we join together and decide what role we want to play to help bridge gaps, so that kids are resilient, open, confident, determined, and free to just be a kid during this precious time of their lives. To contribute and make a difference, that could simply mean having more personal and social awareness, empathy, making a concerted effort to heal ourselves, breaking cycles, or donating our time, attention, and financial support to make sure children have the right to run, have fun, and be free.

Search For Answers

You might find, like many others who've experienced lost innocence, that it can occur child-to-child, adult-to-child, or both, because of things like uninvited sexual experiences, child maltreatment in the home, or child labor violations occurring outside the home. Despite our having been taught early on—through books, TV, or family—to keep ourselves both covered and sacred; our power, bodies, and minds were still stripped away. Unfortunately, millions of children are at risk of experiencing what we once faced, a loss of innocence, at the hands of things like child maltreatment, sex or human-trafficking, and child labor violations.

According to UNICEF, uunless the world tackles these inequities, between now and 2030 there will be about 167 million more children affected. Those living in poverty-stricken areas are the most vulnerable, as they have an adult-child experience and spend their days working, searching, and struggling to get clean water, food, shelter, and financial resources to change their fate.

Feel good knowing this: as we search for answers, understanding, and clarity to grow personally, while we aren't able to save the world all on our own, we can definitely make an effort to take a stand for children, the world around us, and our future. As a result, the world will be not only a better place, but also a safer place for us all to live.

Chapter 4

Looking in the Mirror

Standing in front of the liquor store, with crumpled-up dollars hidden in my hand, I watched and waited, mustering up the courage to ask an adult to buy our alcohol since we were underage.

Scared and worried about getting caught, my friend Keisha reassured me that it would be fine. Then, finally, I did it.

"Excuse me, would you mind buying us a couple of bottles of Boone's Farm if I give you the money?"

"Sure, little mama."

And just like that, alcohol became my drug of choice, with us upgrading to stronger types of alcohol along the way.

I didn't like school or feel comfortable there, so I asked my friends, "Do you want to go? No? Okay, good, let's not go."

So on top of drinking, ditching became the norm, as well as hanging out with guys who didn't always have the best intentions.

I struggled to fit in and find my place. I racked my brain each day on the way to school, trying to devise a plan to figure out how to avoid being easy prey. Asking myself "disempowering" questions like, "What is it about me that makes people want to hurt me?" Naively thinking to myself, "Maybe I should dress like a guy or gain weight to avoid attention."

Secretly I was growing more and more depressed, with thoughts of suicide and self-injury on my mind, but too afraid to actually do anything, and besides, my desire for recognition and validation superseded anything at the time. So much so that it overruled what little sense of judgment I had left, as I ignored my instincts and engaged in unhealthy behaviors and abusive relationships.

Ideally we would be able to take a good long look in the mirror and love what we see, the reflection of ourselves staring back lovingly. However, many of us, after experiencing traumatic events or being exposed to hurt, harm, or danger, tend to have a hard time taking a look in the mirror and liking what we see. Or we find ourselves overly sensitive, critical, or judgmental.

When you're feeling this way, it's hard to live with yourself, to live with what happened, to look at yourself in the mirror. You're ashamed—you can't see your beauty because you are blinded by your emotional pain You're no longer your "happy-go-lucky self," you've been traumatized and are defensive or laugh less. And those around you want the old you back, although something has shifted in you and you don't know how to get it back.

On the other hand, some of us don't have an issue with taking a look in the mirror, but still find that we've suffered a loss of confidence and resiliency, at least temporarily. If you're able to face yourself in the mirror, congratulations for being an exception to the rule!

In my case, there were many events and things that happened up until age eighteen, so much so that I could have easily filled pages and pages with story upon story about my experiences. But this book isn't about me it's about you, with me doing my best to include my stories that are relatable and relevant to you and what you might be going through.

Have you ever felt like you wanted to get better and move forward, but you haven't figured out what to do about it, who to talk to, or how to fix it?

Instead, like me, you're struggling to take a good long look, afraid of what you'll find or what will show up for you?

If you can relate even a little, here's something I do and would like to share with you, in the hope it helps you. Because we are on a journey together, after all, a journey to reclaim your innocence, which in this moment is about learning to reclaim your confidence, starting with your morning and evening routines.

My only disclaimer is that you give yourself permission to be open and willing for the next thirty days, to do this or something similar so it will become second nature.

First, start by taping encouraging words or phrases to your medicine cabinet, bathroom mirror, or on a piece of paper. And if you can't think of any, then for now just use "I am" statements (statements that affirm yourself). Once you have your encouraging words, phrases, or "I am" affirmations, recite them out loud, as you face the mirror.

I know that often looking in the mirror is the hardest part, the part where you need to take a long hard look and begin to speak with love to the person staring back at you, with no condemnation, guilt, shame, or regret.

Here's an example of what I've being doing for years now to increase my confidence, self-love, and to stay positive. And I'm happy to say that I am no longer afraid of the person staring back at me.

Okay, first I give myself a wink, which lightens my mood, gets me going, and makes me laugh and smile. Then I just go with the flow and say whatever comes up and out for that day: "I am L.J," "Looking good, girl," "We're in this together," "I am a beautiful work in progress," "I am doing the best I can," "I am smart, we got this," "I am kind," "I am fun-loving," "In this moment, I am being the best I know how to be."

Quite honestly, on the days or weeks that it's easier said than done, I type out a few sentences to encourage my soul and make my heart smile. Now it's your turn to do the same.

Another reason I recommend and believe it's important that you do this is because of something inside of us called "mirror neurons," which basically allow us to mimic the feelings and emotions of what we see. They can be feelings and emotions in a movie, television show, a person standing in front of us, or the person staring back at us in the mirror (ourselves). So that's why placing your mantras and affirmations on the mirror in your bathroom and repeating them as you look yourself in the eye will help them to sink in both visually and mentally.

One thing I do and suggest for you is to have fun, like an innocent child, making it a daily game, habit, and ritual as if you were watching your favorite show or cheering for your favorite player or actress. In other words, you can be loud, silly, and playful, without caring what anyone else thinks in that moment. The point is, our past shapes us, but doesn't have to rule or define who we are today.

"If you want to see the truth, you must be brave enough to look. –Rune Lazuli

Assessing the Damage

First, we need to recognize that it's a process and decide where we are in the process and understand, our personal journey to increase self-love, growth, and healing doesn't happen overnight. So it's okay to take things slowly and do your best to make educated choices, and not just take an ill-informed guess, especially when you've experienced loss or betrayal in the past.

Then ask yourself what needs to happen before you can tell your story. Have you assessed the damage and picked up the pieces? If not that's why I wrote this book: to help you, at the very least, asses were you are, and where you would like to be as you prepare to take your voice globally or leave a positive, lasting impact for those around you in a much bigger way.

Surprisingly enough, looking back on things I didn't realize when I was growing up that there were professional experts out there like certified life coaches, counselors, and psychotherapists available to help me until I got training to become one myself. In truth, I definitely would have asked my mom to sign me up had I known. But instead, to cope with the fire and the burglary, among other things, my solution landed me right where I didn't want: as a teen alcoholic.

During one of my trainings, we took a look at the "addicted brain" as it relates to things like drug abuse and alcoholism, and the why and how of people becoming addicted, and what could be done to help. At that time I got a little more clarity about myself, and what I learned surprised me. We took an assessment called, "The 40 Developmental Assets", an assessment that allows you to see what assets you bring with you into your adult life, based on what was given to you by your parents. In short, during this training I discovered that I grew up with only six out of 40 assets, which placed me at a 75% risk factor of being an alcoholic, drug addict, you name it. I later shared this with my mother, to which she replied, "Well if you had six, that means I only had three" because she didn't get much support.

Wow! What a big relief. As crazy as it sounds, I felt a sense of peace from gaining that nugget of clarity. It was a testament to our need to assess the damage we face in our relationships, our homes, our self-love, our hopes, and our dreams after a loss of innocence.

Let me explain what I mean. Our goal in doing this is not to place blame, be martyrs, point fingers or have an excuse for the things we do, but rather to assess the damage for the sake of clarity and understanding ourselves just a bit more. Like when the fire marshal came out to find the cause of the fire, or when the American Red Cross assessed the damage caused by the fire. We assess our childhood to see how it shaped us, to gain clarity on the damage done, and what we bring with us into adulthood. It is not to place blame, but so we can solve the mysteries of our upbringing, gain closure, and move on.

On that note, during my training in counseling and guidance, we were encouraged to seek professional help ourselves and required to complete a minimum of 10 hours of counseling. In fact, I worked with an expert who used the Eye Movement Desensitization and Reprocessing (EMDR) technique, allowing me to revisit my past and sort through everything. So I could asses and uncover what was at the root of my anger, rage, and sadness: eleven years of either experiencing abuse or being a witness to it from the time I was four until I was fifteen, with that abusive relationship acting like lighter fluid for my pain.

This too is my hope for you: that on your journey of personal growth and self-discovery, you will be able to assess the damage and gain clarity about your innocence and what happened to you.

Or if you've already done some work, my desire is that after reading this book you will be able to decide which pathway to take next: working with an expert, attending a group, participating in a virtual program, or purchasing a motivational audio book or CD sets.

Use Your Pain as Fuel

As a young adult in my twenties, I tried to be brave and strong, but there were days when I broke down and couldn't carry on.

Trying to pretend I was fine although I cried almost every day, left me feeling trapped, stuck, and angry. The job I chose placed me in an environment that reinforced and triggered negative emotions and memories. As a result, I had to learn to use my pain as the fuel to be my best and not quit on life or my dreams.

A part of me knew, deep down in my heart, that there was hope even when I couldn't feel it, happiness although I didn't always believe it, and a happy life waiting for me although I couldn't see it.

Therefore, the key is to keep going until your emotional pain no longer controls you. Instead, you control it and use it as fuel to ignite your passions and be your best!

After all, both you and your dreams are worth the time, effort, and investment!

One Step at a Time

The nice thing is that the process of learning to use your pain as fuel to grow and heal only requires one step at a time. That means there's no pressure to rush the process and skip valuable steps.

Let me put it another way. I realize that after experiencing a loss of our innocence, much like what happens in a divorce settlement, we have to learn to separate ourselves and divorce the pain, shame, and guilt as we learn to dissolve and cut all ties with any emotions that are making our lives and relationships irreconcilable.

I know that sometimes taking the first step—or a step at all—can prove to be challenging, which is why it's so important to have some sort of support system—a group, virtual class, or someone you trust and find helpful—to support you in this.

As you explore, do some work to loosen, release, and shift any negative emotions and memories. Leverage your pain, heartache, and betrayal, not to guilt-trip others or hold yourself hostage to the past, but to make better choices, decisions, and actions for your health and emotional wealth's sake.

Tying It All Together

Habitat for Humanity, the Red Cross, and organizations like UNICEF make it their business to go into war-torn countries, homes, and areas to help children and families pick up the pieces and begin again.

In the same way, after a loss of your innocence, confidence, trust, hope, self-worth, or personal power, there's no time like now to pick up the pieces and rebuild where your mind, body, and spirit are fragmented.

Just know that while many intentionally or unintentionally follow the path of unhealthy coping skills and create unhealthy habits such as smoking, being controlling or overbearing, and addicted, bitter, angry, or isolated, you don't have too.

You may remember the king of pop, Michael Jackson. His song, "Man in the Mirror," mimics what we've been talking about here. The part of his song I'm referring to says, "I'm starting with the man in the mirror, I'm asking him to change his ways ... if you want to make the world a better place, take a look at yourself and then make that change." That just about sums it up.

For us, looking in the mirror and facing ourselves is tough, but that's exactly why it's important to do it. Taking a look in the mirror and reciting positive affirmations helps us shift, make changes, and reconnect with the innocent child within. Face who you are, who you wish you were and had hoped you'd be, all while saying positive affirmations or things like "I love you" ... "I love all of you, mind, body, and soul with all your rolls, dips, and curves." Yes, as silly as it sounds, positive affirmations help increase self-love and self-acceptance.

One of the most freeing things you can do is take a good long look at yourself in the mirror. Even if it brings you to tears, say, "We're in this together" and then, like me, give yourself a wink and a smile. At the very least, let out a big sigh and with a deep breath say to yourself, "You have my permission to love me and I agree to love you no matter what you're going through. Despite mistakes, unanswered questions, and heartache, I love you and will do my best to continue too."

At the same time, take a quick look back to assess and see what happened to your innocence and how it shaped who you are today. Remember, no matter what the outcome, you can take inventory and no longer put your personal growth, self-care, and emotional well-being on hold.

One of the best ways to do this is to use your pain as fuel to ignite your dreams and make your: health, wellness, and personal growth, development, and healing a priority.

It all comes down to this: regardless of where you find yourself or what you've done to try to deal with your wounds so far, just know that it can and will get better. If you haven't been able to make sense of it all, now is the time to give yourself that opportunity.

Chapter 5

Picking up the Pieces

I headed down to the locker room. I hated working night-shift plus, driving around at night in the dark was even riskier than during the day. But to do my job, there were times and moments like this where I had no choice, so reluctantly I made my way downstairs and started to change out of my civilian clothes and put on my uniform. Not knowing or expecting anyone else to be there, I opened the door to find Sgt. Jacobs. Oh no! I loved Sgt. Jacobs, but for some reason I was feeling like crap and very emotional. I thought I was going to burst into tears as I changed into my uniform but I didn't want her to see me cry.

The emotional holes in my heart were gnawing at me, and a wave of sadness came crashing in and wouldn't let up, no matter how hard I tried. I needed to keep it together, but the weight was too heavy. I put on my uniform shirt and by the time I put one pant leg on, I broke down.

Big crocodile tears fell hard and fast, like a waterfall, as I began to cry uncontrollably. The harder I tried to keep it together, the worse it got. Sgt. Jacobs rushed to me and said, "What's wrong, Jackson?" And then it all came out as I told her everything about my past, things that I had kept secret and I had planned to take to my grave—about the molestation, rape, and my sadness and emotional pain.

Surprisingly, I felt like a thirty-pound weight was no longer on my shoulders, leaving me feeling lighter. But I wasn't sure what she was going to say or do next, because she was tough. I watched as she rushed to the phone across the room and called the Sheriff's Department Employee Support hotline, a service I didn't even know existed. Wow! What a relief! She handed me the phone and I scheduled an appointment with a law enforcement psychologist, which took my journey toward healing to a whole new level.

In the introduction, I shared how my journey to reclaiming my innocence and power all got started, with me searching for answers to my burning question about innocence and why bad things happen to innocent children.

Having been satisfied with what I found, it was time for me to pick up the pieces and figure out what other burning questions I needed answered, as well as what was next for me professionally.

Like the classic children's storybook character, Humpty Dumpty, putting the pieces of our heart, confidence, and self-love back together again is tough, but doable. During this time there's often misunderstanding, miscommunication, and frustration between you, your loved ones, and anyone in your circle of influence; likely leaving you sometimes wondering why you should even bother or try.

I didn't always realize the effects and impact the fire had on me emotionally and mentally, nor did I understand where my misplaced anger and insecurity came from after the burglaries and sexual abuse. As a result, I lived life allowing fear, worry, anger, shame, and regret to control me and had no clue that help from a professional expert was possible at the time. My pain would rise to the surface, trying to send me a signal that something was off track, but I just put on a happy face and pretended like everything was okay.

There were two other big pieces missing from the jigsaw puzzle of my heart that had to be put back together. First, my "daddy issues," which I didn't want to admit existed especially since I kept hearing that most women have similar issues.

In my mind, that was a label I didn't want to wear, but it was the truth. I barely saw my father or spent time with him during the first sixteen years of my life, and rarely saw him as a young adult. And when I did, he would be inebriated (may he rest in peace).

This left me trying to figure out for years why he didn't make time for me. I even offered to let him come live with me in the house I had bought, but he said there was nothing for him to do out where I lived and he would be bored.

Frustrated and confused, it wasn't until my early thirties that I began to spend more time with him and really get the opportunity to feel his love. Throughout the years, I also learned that it was the loss of his own innocence that had changed him based on three key experiences he had. These included:

1. An unhealthy, "insecure attachment" with my grandfather during my father's childhood;
2. Being asked by coaches to perform sexual favors, which as a passionate and talented football player preparing to go pro crushed him- ; and
3. His mom (my grandmother) dying when I was only nine.

All these traumatic events resulted in a loss of his innocence and power. Despite this, before my dad passed away we were able to spend some quality time together, allowing me to know without a shadow of a doubt that he loved me with all his heart and I was able to put yet another piece of my heart back together again.

The other big piece and baffling question I had for myself was whether there were any good men out there in the world, or any I could trust. When I was growing up there were only one or two around. Most of the men did not set very good examples, leaving me, feeling for the most part that men could not be trusted.

However, slowly but surely, good men started to show up and give me hope through healthy experiences, connections, and relationships with no expectations from me. This gave me clarity, a better perspective, and an understanding that the men I met earlier in my life lacked integrity, took advantage of my innocence, or were acting out a loss of personal power in their own lives. None of these were my problems or issues to solve for them.

I also learned that, due to the unhealthy relationships I saw or experienced in childhood and as a young adulthood, I had spent a lot of my life searching and desiring love in a fear-based emotional state, which only got me that in return. I didn't choose to love for love's sake, just because it was fun or I simply wanted too. I entered into relationships "to be loved" and validated, and not "be love", simply a reflection of love for the other person. This had a negative ripple effect, with me entering into a relationship for one of three reasons: to prove to the ghost of my past (my former abuser) that I was lovable; to escape a life I did not want with marriage as my escape route, and to live up to the pressure of the cultural codes and expectations of the world around me by having children and raising a family (not that there's anything wrong with that). But I am happy to report that I since learned and know the love I was searching for in men can only be found within me.

So now, with all the pieces of my heart's puzzle solved and the holes mended, my hope, desire, and wish is that you are able to do the same.

My hope is that you're already starting to feel a shift after your own inner work, and you are now more self-aware, understanding, and accepting of who you are

To support you on your journey of self-discovery, I have included a questionnaire in the resources section in the back of this book. If you answer any of the questions with a resounding "yes" or even a "maybe," congratulations in advance for being one step closer to reclaiming your innocence and personal power. Plus, this is a simple yet huge step in figuring out where you are and where you want to be.

Honor Your Feelings

I recently interviewed several women and asked them to take time out to honor their feelings, whatever they may be: sadness, anger, regret. However, one of the ladies objected and said that she didn't want to let go of her emotional attachment to her past because she was afraid doing so would send a message that what happened was okay and they were off the hook.

On the contrary, honoring our feelings and emotions is important and necessary in order for us to validate and acknowledge what happened, release it, and let go or loosen its grip on our lives.

As human beings, we are naturally wired together and designed in such a way that something deep down inside of us knows:

- When our spirit is not at rest
- We haven't let something go
- We haven't processed our feelings and emotions

In essence, when we don't take time out to honor our feelings and emotions, it's like we are ignoring our heart's song, internal compass, or our GPS system leaving our sense of direction and understanding less than what it could be, As a result, unless we take time to grow personally and mature emotionally we lack a greater sense of resiliency and improved coping skills.

Here's another way to look at the benefits of honoring of feelings. When we get the news of a loved one or friend passing away, we are emotionally moved to respond. Usually, the closer we are to them, the more it hurts us, upsets us, saddens us, and makes us want to give our condolences and pay our respects. As we allow our emotional tears to help us release emotionally, calm down, and relax after crying and getting it out.

In the same way, our lost innocence has created the loss of a very special part of us, gone way to soon. So when we take time out to do this, it gives us the opportunity to acknowledge and pay our respects to our pain, grief, anger, hurt, rage, or whatever else we're feeling. This allows the innocent child within to release the emotional pressure and lift the weight of carrying the toxic emotions inside. This can decrease the risk of stress-related illness. Research studies, hospitals, and treatment centers are proof that the alternative to not taking time out to honor our feelings increases the potential for things like: road rage, substance abuse (alcohol, drugs), an increase of suicidal thoughts, or mental breakdowns (panic attacks, anxiety, depression) just to name a few.

Post-Traumatic Grief

Many people find it easier to honor their anger or rage than their grief or sadness, and I believe societal norms and cultural codes have a lot to do with that. In fact, many people dishonor the healing or grieving process simply because of the pressure of an invisible timeline placed on the length of time they have to grieve. Often they are pressured to hurry up and move on because it makes someone around them uncomfortable.

Other people see sadness or taking time out to grieve as a sign of weakness. This can be based on comments made by someone in your family when you were young; or things like TV shows, movies, and the media with messages like:

- "Don't get all emotional on me"
- "You're being too emotional"
- "Stop crying like a baby."

From my experience, both personally and professionally, our grief is equally important to recognize, pay attention to, and acknowledge.

For my eighteenth birthday, we had a combined mother's day and birthday brunch. I really wanted to enjoy everyone around me, feel good, and be happy, but I still felt sad and disappointed with myself and life, wondering if this was all there was. During the brunch I expressed my concerns to a family member as tears began to roll down my cheeks. She then rattled off a list of all the reasons why I should be happy: "You have a good job, you have a car, and you're in college getting your education."

Like many other people I realized and knew deep down inside, those outer things are not enough. But to make everyone around us feel comfortable, we often settle or put on an emotional mask and play a role. This happens far too often and more than it should for millions of people today, leaving people on an emotional roller coaster that they want to get off of, but just don't know how.

Here's what I discovered and what I realized after receiving tons of training, degrees, and certifications, as well as after working with hundreds and hundreds of people.

People are not only experiencing Post-Traumatic Stress Disorder (PTSD), but they are also showing symptoms of what I call *Post-traumatic Grief (PTG).*

Allow me to explain further. In recent years, social awareness has helped bring attention to, and an understanding of PTSD and its negative effects that occur as a result of: exposure to, experiencing, or witnessing very traumatic or life-threatening events.

In fact, according to the World Health Organization and many like it, both adults and children suffer with PTSD. According to psychiatrist and brain specialist Dr. Daniel Amen's book, Making a Good Brain Great (2005), PTSD stems from things like "physical and sexual abuse, terror, accidents, threats, combat, and witnessing things that shock our system and the wiring in our brain after traumatic events." In short, if left untreated, PTSD can ruin lives and even lead to suicide.

That being said, Post-traumatic Grief (PTG) is similar to Post traumatic Stress (PTSD) in that, it takes place after things like physical and sexual abuse, witnessing or experiencing traumatic events that shock our system. However, the type of emotional triggers that need to be addressed are different. For example, instead of being stress induced (post-traumatic stress), PTG is "grief" induced (post-traumatic grief), meaning that the negative effects of Post-Traumatic Grief stem from things like neglected or unattended grief. This is grief that happens on an emotional, mental, or cellular level after experiencing a loss of someone or something valuable, and in our case a loss of our innocence.

To explain further, while they both have a lot in common one big difference lies in that PTSD has an emphasis on the *stress* that takes place after a traumatic event or threat of danger, which in turn causes things like: shock, distress, and alarm. PTG has an emphasis on the *grief,* which leads to the: heartache, sadness, and unhappiness we face after the *loss* of a person, place, thing, or idea we once shared, valued, or cherished being suddenly ripped away.

What does this mean for you? Well, while knowing this helps us take time out to deal with our grief, it can also change a family's dynamic and legacy. It can also help us with our own children or the children around us because they are like sponges and tend to act out what they see going on with the loved ones or adults around them. So in making an effort to heal your PTG on a cellular, emotional, and mental level, you are demonstrating, modeling, and giving others permission to heal theirs too.

Something to also be aware of is the need to understand the benefits and importance of grief and the grieving process, because by doing so we gain clarity and feel better. This is why Elisabeth Kübler-Ross' *Five Stages of grief & Loss from her book on Death and Dying, 1969* (along with variations of it) continue to be a powerful process used across the globe to help people make sense of how they feel and the emotions they experience after the death of a loved one.

So whether you ceremoniously acknowledge and validate your past emotions prior to laying them to rest as I talk about in this chapter, or you decide to utilize Elisabeth's five stage process: denial, anger, bargaining, depression/sadness, and acceptance. What's important to know is the key to healing is going through the process of getting things up and out, which in turn allows the executive functioning of our brain to get back to doing its job of clear-thinking.

If you find yourself still having a challenging time letting go of something your parents did (or didn't do) when you were young, like me, maybe it will help if you symbolically released and laid to rest the parents you wished they would have been, so you can appreciate them just as they are now.

Here are some examples of what doing so looks like:

- Have a ceremonial release in your mind
- Go outside and release balloons or a sky lantern
- Journal, cry, and say goodbye to the parents you imagined, wished, and hoped for.

Bottom-line, most parents do the best they know how, which may not be "the best", but it was "their best" at the time. The most important things is for you to do whatever will allow you to let go so you can start to enjoy life more and more. No longer chained, trapped, or bound to old stories and patterns that have had a hold on you.

Responses and Actions of Others

The responses and actions of others around you can vary and be anywhere from completely empathetic, supportive, and understanding to insensitive, callous, and cruel. Whatever the case, I encourage you to keep *going* and keep *growing* despite the responses, actions, and opinions of others.

A few years back, I attended a networking event where we agreed to form accountability partners to support one another in our business endeavors. As I began to tell my accountability partner about my goals and plans to help women increase their confidence, happiness, and self-esteem so they can achieve their dreams. She interrupted me and said, "'Help?' My advice to you is that you make it a point to not use the word 'help' at all, because to me the word help is a sign of weakness- so I suggest you use a word like, "support" instead.

Initially, I took her advice to heart and started to identify what other words I could use to describe the work that I do. But the more I thought about it, the more I realized that the word "help" is actually the perfect word to describe what I've done for the past two decades, and plan to do for years to come. Why? The word "help" is a universal word understood in every language to signify a need for assistance or show that there's a situation or event taking place that can't be solved on one's own.

When my family and I were trapped alive in the burning house, we weren't worried about being seen or viewed as weak for asking for help. In fact, our desire to get out of the situation we were in was much more important than anything else at that time. Just imagine the difference in response had I decided my ego and what others may think was more important in that moment of vulnerability or "weakness" as some see it. I know it sounds kind of silly, but can you picture me jumping out of the tub and shouting, "Support, support ... somebody support me" instead of "Help, help ... somebody help me". When you think about it, the word "support" suggests and sends a different message to others.

My point being, I want you to feel confident in knowing that your time is now, and on your journey of personal growth and healing it's okay to make your needs known and be loud and proud to ask for help.

Your innocence matters, your feelings matter, and so does, doing whatever it takes to get it back and reclaim your power.

It all comes down to this: along the way, there will be people who will project their opinions, thoughts, and believes on you for whatever reasons. Your value, self worth, and self-love are not based on the opinions and judgments of others, regardless of what's happened to you.

Casualties of Loss

Looking back, when I was fifteen years old, I tried to reach out for help in my own way by telling my friends how abusive Tony was to me. Unfortunately, their advice during that time was for me to get over it and not to make anything of it as they said things like " he doesn't mean any harm, he just loves you a lot" I mention this because a lack of understanding of what love is, and isn't or what abuse is, or isn't is often the root cause of why we don't leave an unhealthy relationship right away.

Maybe, like me, no matter how hard you've tried to have a positive attitude and outlook on life, you find it hard to get over it due to the casualties of your loss.

Here are the top six scenarios or challenges clients have expressed at the start of our work together. I wanted to share them with you so you can identify and begin to put a name to the things you are feeling and experiencing if you haven't already done so.

1. You want to feel better and be different, but you don't know how and no one seems to understand what you're going through.

2. You're under pressure to perform, to keep up, meet expectations, fit in, and belong. A part of you wishes everyone would just leave you alone, at the same time you're lonely and feel invisible or ignored. It's all a façade and you're tired of feeling like a phony, but you don't know what else to do to get through.
3. Everything looks foggy and unclear, and you feel powerless to change your situation or circumstances. Your faith in yourself and in humanity has changed. All hope for your life and dreams seem uncertain.
4. You're on an emotional roller coaster ride, unsure how you got there, how to get off, or how to explain what you're feeling from day-to-day.
5. You're tired and you don't know what else to do so you drown your sorrows by over-consuming (food, sex, drugs, or alcohol) and now both your emotional and financial bank accounts are bleeding.
6. Confrontations are your forte. Your defense mechanisms are in full throttle. Your adrenal glands have worked over time, almost nonstop since childhood, and now all you want is peace and safety without the need to be "always on" all the time.

You may identify with these scenarios. It may still be hard to let go and move on, or you may find that you've managed to succeed in some aspects of life, but something is still missing or not quite right. Maybe you feel fragmented, scattered, and limited.

Know that the quickest way for your head and your heart to heal is by facing it straight on. So don't just "go" through the motions as you read this book and complete the questionnaire. Instead reflect, ponder, and think things through making it a point to put something you've learned into action

Tying It All Together

One of my personal philosophies and beliefs is that I didn't survive and overcome all that I have just to spend the rest of my days unhappy, angry, or depressed all the time. No. Instead, I'm convinced that my job is to laugh as loud as I can, for as long as I can, and as much as I can, like an innocent child doing my best to not take myself or life too seriously—although sometimes I still do.

You may be at a place in your life where you need to appreciate your innocence, realize your need to pick up the pieces, honor your feelings, or acknowledge your post-traumatic grief.

Whatever the case, know and understand that the goal of revisiting, discussing, and facing your past is to do so not as a martyr, but rather as a fully empowered and aware person taking a temporary step back. Honoring your feelings, emotions, and grief as a necessary part of the healing and letting go process.

What should you do when your painful past is just an "oh well" response to the people around you or those who harmed you? You work with an expert you trust to give you a safe space to help, guide, coach, mentor, or support you. If that is not right for you participate in activities that help you let go and release. At the very least, when it's safe to do so, take a five-to-fifteen-minute mental break. Then be still, and trust that in the quiet stillness ideas and answers will start to reveal themselves to you as you think about your current situation, reflect, and journal about whatever it is you've been holding on too.

By knowing better, you can now do better as you move forward, loving yourself and experiencing healthy connections and relationships without fear, simply for love's sake. As you leverage your past, you can permanently stop wearing a mask, and use your internal GPS and compass so you can have a great life despite everything.

Remember the most important thing right now is to determine what pieces you need to put back together to start anew.

Chapter 6

Reclaim Your Innocence

I met jessica at one of my speaking engagements. During my talk, she grabbed her phone and started looking something up. I wasn't sure what had become such a distraction for her, but I continued to talk and encourage the women in the room. After my talk, I found out that she was looking up my website, excited about the opportunity to work together. We talked briefly and scheduled a phone conversation so that we could talk more and make sure that she was serious and ready to take action as a coaching client.

During her phone consultation, she proceeded to share and talk at great length. She was successful by the world's standards, well respected in her community, an avid traveler, loved to cook, and spend time with her friends and family. I wasn't sure what issues she faced, but I knew from our earlier conversation that something was secretly bothering her. She then told me about her experience of lost innocence after being betrayed by two people she loved most.

As a result, she shared that she was sad, self-protective, holding back, bitter, afraid of success, attracting the wrong men, and afraid of putting herself out there at the risk of getting hurt. Although she was extremely loyal to others, she was making a concerted effort to keep people at a distance. This was a story I was all too familiar with, personally and now professionally.

After discussing options, programs, and services, she decided to sign up for my six-month program exclusively for women, with a goal of: gaining self-awareness, creating boundaries, increasing her confidence, and happiness, as well as several career goals.

She also was looking to grow and learn how to say "no" to others because she had a habit of being a rescuer, enabler, and self-sacrificing.

Quite honestly challenges showed up that left her tempted to not do the work or take the action steps needed to get results. But six months later she expressed gratitude and appreciation, and said she could feel that she was self-evolving, felt good about her progress with her goals, and was in the process of transitioning in her career. Plus, she said having accountability and space to talk things through and not have to be the strongest one in the room made a difference.

I share her story with you because I often hear this a lot: women say they're the strongest one in their family, are over committed, stressed, or struggle with boundaries. Women have also expressed that although they can relate, and they'd be my ideal client, they wouldn't want to admit it in front of others and in some cases even to themselves. My response to that is true evolution is self-evolution and occurs when we, as human beings, become more than we were before. if you're not ready for one-on-one services, your next step can simply be to join a group, online course, or virtual program. The beauty of our personal power is that we all have a voice and choice to decide.

The most important thing to remember is that the journey we are on allows us to return home to our true, authentic selves and reclaim what's rightfully ours- our innocence. Like when we were young and we lived life from a "heart-minded" space, not perfect, yet innocent.

In fact, innocence symbolizes and represents who we all have the potential to be, at the core of our being (before innocence was lost): giving, trusting, wholesome, hopeful, faithful, honest, fun, and confident.

The bottom line is: innocence is not the sum of our experiences at any given level of our childhood, but rather the potential and ability to grow personally, heal emotionally, and tap into our creativity all the days of our life. As you also tap into your "personal rights" to not spend your days: insecure, depressed, anxious, as a workaholic, or uptight, stiff-necked adult who takes herself way to serious unless you want too.

That being the case, taking time out to reclaim your innocence isn't about going from one extreme to the other either: putting yourself in harm's way, being naïve, letting your guard down unsafely, or feeling silly or overly animated either. Rather, it's no longer holding yourself or those around you captive to a life less than it would be had your innocence not been lost and changed things.

In the spirit of innocence, you can put an adult spin on childhood fun. Or take it a step further by making a commitment to select one activity in each area: physically, emotionally, and mentally. However, remember you get to decide what works for you. Here are some ideas to get you started:

1. Reclaim your innocence physically

Jog, engage in exercise, play tag/freeze, play a sport, play video games, read comics or books, play with toys and board games, color in adult coloring books, draw/paint, skip, jump rope, or go on an adventure, explore, hike, bike, skate, jump on a trampoline (kid or adult version). Quite honestly, the possibilities are endless.

2. Reclaim your innocence emotionally

Laugh, affirm yourself, engage in emotionally stimulating conversations, learn to shift your thinking, practice be able to shift your mindset so you feel good, happy, content, grateful, and capable of being at peace.

These are a few examples to help you get started and should be geared toward your personality.

3. Reclaim your innocence mentally

Be resilient, determined, confident, take chances, see the world with childlike wonder, and get involved in new projects, relationships, connections, and interactions,.

Additionally, another thing we can do to reclaim our innocence is to obtain new or "earned secure attachments" in the healthy connections and relationships we have now. Other activities you can do to reclaim you innocence include renting or going to children's movies by yourself or taking out a piece of paper and scribbling on the page.

Bottom line: doing something creative allows you to get out of your left brain and get into the creative part of your right brain, which is very liberating.

It also sends a message to the innocent child within you that she hasn't been forgotten, and although you are an adult with adult responsibilities, you will make it a goal to have play dates with yourself and just run, have fun, and be free.

Care plans

At the very least, take care of yourself, which is something as children we kind of just did. We got up, got dressed, and the focus of the day was what we were going to do and what we were going to eat.

About three or four years ago, I spent two weeks working at two elementary schools, something I hadn't done in years. So I brushed up on my art therapy and ways to help young children. As I was taking a look at my books and intervention handouts, I came across something really cool. It was a handout in one of my books called the "Comfort Kit", which was a simple but great way to make sure my clients of any age took care of themselves. The basic premise or idea was to take a brown paper bag and place food and snack items, along with things that would provide you with comfort, in the event of a hard day or even a crisis.

After reviewing it, I made a note and decided to create a more mature version with a twist with my adult clients in mind called the "Care Plan." Let's take a closer look. Whether you decide to engage in fun and innocent activities, make yourself a comfort kit, a Care Plan, or you choose to do something totally different, it's up to you. Just remember the goal is to help you to heal, grow, and keep the highest level of self-care as it relates to reclaiming your innocence.

Whatever the case, make sure you have an overall game plan for ways to bounce back permanently, completely, and wholeheartedly. So your Care Plan should include ways to care for yourself mentally, physically, and emotionally likewise.

The nice thing about creating your Care Plan is that you can also have your very own cheerleading squad, which includes a few trusted family, friends, and mentors who can cheer for you when you find it hard to cheer for yourself. You can also decide in advance if you want to make it fun by having your very cheerleading squad come up with their own cheers and chants for you, or you can give them hints on words, phrases, and songs that speak to your heart or actions like high fives that really can make a difference.

No Care Plan should be without Vitamin D, unless it's not a safe haven out or you have a skin condition that doesn't allow you to be in the sun. Your plan should definitely include getting some sunlight, being one with nature, and enjoying scenic views around you. If that's just not possible, you can draw or buy a picture of flowers or a scenic view and keep it in a book or put it on your wall.

Last, but not least, your Care Plan should include things to eat that boost both your mood and your mind in healthy ways. It should also include affirmations, mantras, and meditations, as well as prayers if you're a person who likes to pray. These serve to help ground and anchor you and the innocent child within knowing that as a responsible, mature adult it's possible to be a child at heart when life allows.

Redefine Moments

Now that you've taken care of yourself, it's time to look within and redefine moments, situations, and circumstances that are interfering and getting in the way.

By definition, redefining moments is about assigning a new meaning or different definition to something that's happened, hence the word "redefining"

Like when I mentioned earlier that we can ask ourselves "empowering" or "disempowering' questions. In the same way, we can redefine moments and instances in our lives in such a way that we're left feeling like powerful overcomers, instead of powerless victims. Looking back, when I initially sought help for myself, the expert I worked with suggested I redefine or "reframe" my feelings, emotions, and past trauma so I could be at peace and move on. But in my mind, how could I?

At that time in my life, I just didn't get it, although I wanted too. Back then the picture inside my head of everything that happened wasn't a pretty one. It was like one giant inkblot. I couldn't understand why I would want to redefine or reframe something so tragic, repackage something so painful in a nice pretty bow, or wrap it in words that were positive. I just wasn't there yet.

The longer I live and the more I work with clients, the more I understand the benefits and importance of taking time out to redefine old thoughts and reframe past conversations or situations that hurt us.

Knowing what I know now, I would tell the younger me to: see life as a journey, a beautiful song, and the best movie ever to make it on the big screen. I would tell her that she's playing the leading role and acquiring the best tips, tools, insights, and techniques along the way.

If you had the chance to speak to a younger version of yourself, what would you say?

If I could send an instant message to all the women of the world, I would say, "Along the way your mission is to heal and restore what was once sacred, lost, or stripped away. Know that you are: learning to communicate effectively, creating healthy boundaries, and cope with style, and in each moment you're doing your best! Understand that you need not be in the company or space of anyone who used or abused you, or zaps you of your energy."

Acceptance and Understanding

As part of my own personal introspection, I have come to accept and understand several things about myself. I increase my risk of making decisions I'll later regret or run the risk of making the same mistakes twice when I let my ego lead me and run the show or I act on impulse. I also realize that in most cases: had my emotional intelligence been higher and my courage to communicate my needs and wants been more rock solid- things would have been different growing up. That being said, I also realize it's the sum total of all my experience that has made me the woman I am today. For that reason, I am now a lifelong learner on a passionate quest to help improve the lives of others along the way. Like fine wine: fermenting each day, brewing patiently, improving in quality consistently, and sprouting into something beautiful daily.

That is something I hope and desire for you too! May you accept yourself completely, come to understand your past meaningfully, and gain clarity to navigate your life's journey powerfully and freely. To help you be able to live and enjoy the rest of your life, and see it turn out better than you ever thought it would despite what you've gone through.

Climbing Up and Out

When firefighters set out to fight a fire, they have to decide what tools they need, as well as which ladders to use. They have many options to choose from, so the real question is what type of ladder is needed when they are attempting to save a life.

In the same way, our amygdala store and holds on to all the memories we've ever had. These memories don't go away, at least not on their own, so every time we have a new experience, conversation, or interaction these stored memories play a role in influencing the feelings and emotions we assign to these new events (for better or worse). So when we are attempting to climb up and out and heal, the best ladder to use to get to our amygdale will require that we use what I call, the emotional ladder of our brain.

Here's how to understand each part of this ladder:

- The upper part or step of our brain's ladder is where we do our higher-level of thinking and execute goals and plans, etc.
- The next part or step of our brain's ladder is where our emotions, drives, memories, emotional reactions, etc..
- The bottom part or step of our brain's ladder is where is focused on getting our basic needs met (i.e. food, water, shelter, clothing)

So the key to climbing up and out is to figure out what step in your emotional ladder needs to be focused on first. Or what chapter in this book speaks to you most and will help you grow up just a little bit more and help you find balance you seek.

To put it another way, *the Fires of life* happen to us all, often leaving us with: trouble focusing, feeling discouraged, a lost sense of direction, with life or our future at a standstill. This results in a need for an escape route, exit plan, fire escape, or in this case- our emotional ladder as a way to climb up and out of current habits, relationships, careers, etc.

Tell Your Story

During a radio interview, someone asked me to share another key ingredient I believed was critical in the process of personal growth and healing and what I realized as I thought about it for a few minutes may surprise you.

After working with people of all walks of life, ages, and generations, from the smallest child to the biggest, toughest adult is that people need to share their personal story fully before they can let go of past hurt, trauma, and drama. Here's what I mean, when people often instinctively repeat their story to anyone who'll listen, it's because their voices were never heard or they were misunderstood or disrespected. As a result, they never really obtained closure and they talk about it like it happened yesterday, when it could have happened decades ago.

Regardless of color, gender, religion, culture, or financial status—everyone wants to: feel respected, heard, and appreciated.

So that's why it's a key ingredient that many people seek and benefit from when working with a life coach, counselor, or therapist who support storytelling and provides a safe space for clients to share their personal story with dignity.

That being said, telling your story to a trained expert is different than telling your story to a friend or family member. Here's why. When we share our story informally, we often do so with a different purpose in mind: to vent our frustrations, get someone to side with us, or explain why something or someone is bothering us. However, when we share our story with an expert, the goal is often to gain clarity and insight about the different aspects of our life, and then create an action plan. Or get help to shift our mindset and deal with negative thoughts, habits, and memories from our early childhood-memories still stored in our amygdala, just harder to recall later in life. These emotional memories play an instrumental part in causing us to engage in things like emotional eating, emotional spending, shopping or gambling. This puts us at greater risk of being involved in unhealthy or unsatisfying intimate relationships, while trying to fill a void that can only be filled from within. We settle for careers or jobs less than we had hoped, wanted, or desired; or buy superficial things to prove our value and worth. There is also a risk of being too cautious in life or afraid to take any chances.

That's why a key ingredient for personal growth and healing is telling your story to a trained expert, so you can process and release memories and redefine them. This frees us so that we can make the best possible choices, decisions, and actions in our careers, relationships, finances, and life based on what we now know about our innocence, and our memories. This also allows us to give ourselves permission to create a new and positive story for ourselves.

Then share your story with those who want to listen and whom it will inspire. Despite what happened in your past, you're going to be your best. Make it your goal to release negative memories and emotions that served you then but have no place in your life now. Our brain stores memories from birth on. We may not be able to recall every single memory we have, but that doesn't mean they are not there. So of bottom line importance is a releasing these memories on a cellular, mental, and emotional level, which will not only release them, but also release their power in your life.

Forgive yourself

Often times, our old story is based in situations or circumstances where someone hurt us or betrayed our trust. While it's important to work to forgive them as part of our healing process, "we can't give what we don't have". So we must first start with forgiving ourselves.

Holding ourselves, or the innocent child within us, bondage to past actions, choices, and decisions leaves little time to enjoy the present and reduces hope for the future. So taking time out and giving ourselves the space to feel and grieve allows us to gain increased awareness. It also gives us the opportunity to calm our mind, quiet the voices (negative self-talk/inner critic) and eases our heart. At the same time giving the innocent part of us the chance to realign, make peace, and begin to heal and move on spiritually, emotionally, and mentally.

Forgiving ourselves not only lets us off the hook, but it also releases us from the false belief and idea that we have to be perfect or can't make mistakes. And at the risk of sounding cliché, sometimes doing so simply requires understanding that "hindsight is 20/20" and "hindsight with insight" is even better. In other words, we did our best with the information we had at the time so there's no need to beat ourselves up or blame ourselves for something we can't take back.

Other times forgiving yourself will require redefining childhood memories to help you understand that much of what happened was out of your control and rested on the shoulders of those who betrayed your trust and need help with their own issues.

Here's something you can do to get started to help you on your journey of forgiveness:

- Write a letter to yourself as if you were talking to a young, innocent child (naïve, lacking knowledge, trusting) and sincerely want them to forgive themselves for mistakes they've made.

OR

- Write a poem or card to yourself as if you were lovingly attempting to encourage your own: child, cousin, niece, nephew, or relative, to inspire them and teach them about forgiveness.

If by chance, you find forgiveness and acceptance hard or easier said than done, just know that it may take time for both your head and your heart to catch up. It's only a matter of time before you are able to get from where you are to where you want to be. You may need to start with an activity that engages both your head and your heart in the process on a deeper level. Try starting with an emotional release by doing the following:

1. Set your cell phone or watch for 15 minutes
2. Then with the intention of releasing pinned up emotions (i.e. fear, anger, sadness).
3. Free write on a piece of paper or in your journal, writing down any and every thought that comes to mind during this time.
4. After your 15 minutes is up, read what you wrote to see what came up and if there is a common thread.
5. Then say something like, "I now release you and your attachment to me".

Doing activities like this creates space to perform "heart surgery", figuratively speaking, as we open up our heart and remove emotional blockage that would have otherwise not be cleared.

That being said if you found some deep-rooted issues, from severe trauma, that rose to the surface, and you're ready to address them. You might want to consider seeking an expert trained in Eye Movement Desensitization and Reprocessing (EMDR) technique, Cognitive-Behavior therapy (CBT), or Neuro-Linguistic Programming (NLP), techniques that can help loosen or release your trauma and the negative emotions tied to them.

However, if you find yourself uncertain or not quite ready to go that deep, just be sure to do something that brings you one step further. You can start by asking yourself, "What's one small step I am willing to take today after reading this book?" Here are a few example options:

- Complete the questionnaire in the back of this book
- Join L.J.'s 7 week "reclaimed innocence" virtual program for more help and support at www. reclaimedinnocence.com
- Tune-in to the Wise Up and Rise Up radio show for weekly inspiration and tips at www.wiseupandriseupradio.com).

Whatever you decide, remember you are the expert of your own life so you get to determine what's next for you.

In the famous words of Paul D. Tripp, "No one is more influential in your life than you are, because no one talks to you more than you do." So at the very least, remember to speak life into your head and your heart: fan dormant hopes, dreams, and esteem into a flame as you use mantras, affirmations, and positive self-talk to create a healthier outlook about how you view, feel, and see yourself.

Tying It All Together

I am still amazed when I think to myself, "Who knew my past childhood pain would allow me to help thousands of people since then?" As I think back, it's been a humbling, happy, and fun experience helping others achieve their dreams and experience breakthroughs and take action to make their dreams happen. But I never would have guessed it years ago. So I am both thankful and grateful that I didn't allow my emotional pain to get the best of me or keep me from living and experiencing what was waiting for me on the other side.

Now it's your turn to take care of you and allow yourself to reclaim your innocence. No longer pretending and masking your pain. Know this: forgiving yourself and redefining moments that once defined you and stripped you of your innocence will also help you in your journey of moving forward, purposefully and powerfully unabated.

Tell your story and when you're done, create a new empowering one. As you provide yourself with an opportunity to tap into your emotional ladder so you can: *feel, deal, and heal* as part of the journey on the road of personal growth. In this way, the innocent child within you can begin to let go, knowing she doesn't have to hide her feelings anymore.

This is a simple yet powerful way to take back what's innately yours physically, mentally, and emotionally!

Chapter 7

Reclaim Your Power

Jennifer was a client of mine who grew up during a time when it was a cultural norm for parents to have their children pretty much raise themselves. Jennifer's parents made sure her basic needs for food, shelter, and clothing were met. For one reason or another, both her mother and father were emotionally unavailable, worked around the clock, and at times just were too self-absorbed to take time to nurture her.

As a result, Jennifer had to figure things out on her own and unfortunately like many, went through puberty alone, receiving sex education informally from the neighborhood boys. She was also responsible for her siblings, in between chores and homework, so she didn't have much of a social life growing up. Jennifer wanted to be popular and belong, but just when things got settled, her family moved again and she had to change schools.

She was exhausted and tired of all the responsibilities placed on her by her family. So she married young in order to move out of her parents' house and from under their tight grip.

By the time Jennifer and I met, she told me that she felt powerless, worthless, and lacked confidence to pursue her dreams. But she was also determined to pursue her goals and dreams and create a new story for herself.

Although nervous about leaving her job after ten years of working there, she knew that it was time to step out of her comfort zone. However, she admitted to feeling scattered and needed help and direction to figure out where to begin and how to set things in motion. So we had a session by phone and I was able to help her organize her goals and map out a personalized action plan to get started.

Truthfully, as I was typing out Jennifer's story to share with you, at least half a dozen other women came to mine who share her story (partially or completely). I also couldn't help but think about the fact that her story is the story for entire generations of people. Take the men and women of "Generation X" for instance, which consist of approximately 88 million people born 1961–1981, many of which grew up "latch key": innocent, lacking guidance, raising themselves, clueless about money management, and things like healthy coping skills. According to research, now in their forties and struggling with things like paying bills, and often struggling to demonstrate emotional and financial intelligence in life, business, and love.

After working with Millenial's over the course of a ten year period, I can't help but see commonalities between these two generations.

In fact, there appears to have been an unintentional ripple effect or generational cycles created... when Baby Boomers were uninvolved or less involved in their role of raising Generation X'ers, who then passed on to Millenial's (Generation Y) much of what they experienced. Now Millenial's are faced with watching their younger brothers and sisters, relatives, or even their own children struggle with the same five areas: relational (intimate and personal), financial, personal (life and career), emotionally, and spiritual. As a result, millions upon millions of people, across multiple generations, have both a need and desire to get help with ways to reclaim their personal power.

Types of Power

Over the years, I've come to understand one simple rule: we all have a voice and a choice (whether it's being stifled or not), which is why reclaiming your innocence and reclaiming your power go hand in hand.

One thing I want to stress is that there are different types of power, and as such, there are variations of our personal power. One important caveat I want to mention is that we're not referring to power as it pertains to authority, control, coercion, force, tyrants, or dictators.

Rather, this power is our God-given personal power that I define as—the power to use your voice and choice to decide what you will do, think, and be. This God-given personal power is ours based on the simple fact that we are all human beings and we all have the same innate, inner strength to use our voice and choice. We all can decide what we will do, think, and be in life at any given moment, without the desire to harm others or allow our ego to run the show.

However, what typically happens is that, as children, we are often either ill equipped to use our personal power or find ourselves unable to fully use this power. This is due to being considered a minor and therefore unable to be completely independent of adult control (unless we emancipate ourselves and are able to show that we have what it takes to do so). To be fair, sometimes as children we lack the maturity to make wise decisions with our personal power, so adults around us feel the need to step in and take away our ability to choose for ourselves. Another important caveat to mention is that sometimes it's not our parents who inhibit us from tapping into our personal power, but rather societal norms and conditioning.

Reclaiming your power matters because we were born for more, and the fact that you woke up this morning is confirmation of your worth and that you're meant to be here. In spite of everything that's happened, from being carried in your mother's womb up until now, we were not put here to live an unhappy or shattered life. Despite how you may feel or what thoughts are going through your head, you were born for more!

To go for more, you have to do something to move you forward. To move myself forward, I read books, signed up for events, and workshops recommended to me or that I thought would help me. During that time, I attended a workshop with women from around the globe, and began to realize that what I went through was a universal story and common for many women. As other women shared about their past experiences, I also learned that despite outward appearances, we're not alone and we're not the only one.

The Power of Saying No and Setting Boundaries

I also learned to say "no" and set boundaries because at one point, I didn't really have any or thought no one would listen anyway. This was, in short, the power to decide, say "no," and set boundaries, which allow you to set limits or limitations on what's okay and not okay in a positive way.

If you've ever seen young children in a movie preparing to fight, they usually start by saying something to the effect of, "Cross this line, I dare you," or draw a line in the dirt or sand. The point is that boundaries allow us to tap into our personal power and use our voice and choice to decide whom to let into our personal, emotional, and mental space. It also helps us be brave enough to decide who to trust with that space, or who to invite in or out of that space as we move forward.

Boundaries are not only spatial or physical, but there are also emotional boundaries, relationship boundaries, and communication boundaries whereby we learn to say "no". Saying "no" isn't about being mean, it's about the limits we set on how much we disclose about ourselves and our lives when we meet someone for the first time, or are still getting to know them, their heart and level of integrity.

In fact, years ago during a wonderful training I received as a clinical and school-based counselor, we discussed boundaries as they pertain to the level of communication one normally engages in with a stranger, acquaintance, or friend. In general we don't and shouldn't tell all of our business to a complete stranger, as it may be: too much for them to handle, too much too soon, or something that neither one of us really should discuss with the other.

To be clear, one of our main goals is to always find balance between having childlike wonder, hope, faith, and curiosity mixed with proper boundaries, which may take some getting used to.

Like many of us, you may have grown up being told or hearing some variation of things like, "Children are to be seen not heard," "What goes on in this house stays in this house," "Don't put our business in the street," and "Stop crying, get over it, and don't tell anyone." It's conversations and interactions like these that play in our mind later on if we're not careful and forget to say things like, "My inner critic doesn't define me" as we go about our life, careers, and relationships. Remember, no matter how old we are or who we are, the best way to reclaim our power (at this stage of life) is to do so by keeping, maintaining, and tapping into boundaries.

The Power of Instincts

Naturally, after taking a look at the power of boundaries, we should also take a look at, and respect the power of our instincts. You know that gut feeling, sixth sense, or voice that speaks to you about people and places, leaving you with a sense of whether or not they are safe or you should be around or near them. Some people say positive and negative vibes, energy, or frequencies are one in the same, while others say these things help us to be in tune with our instincts and listen more often.

In either case, our instincts help keep us safe as we learn more and more and become a better judge of others' characters. People show us who they are more by what they do and less by what they claim. In truth, in this way we reclaim our innocence, and reclaim our power by recognizing when certain people or environments aren't safe or healthy, and making the necessary changes to these as swiftly and quickly as we can without feeling guilty.

The good news is, we can break free, transform, and create a positive ripple effect in our lives. And in the words of Maya Angelou, in the meantime, "Do the best you can until you know better, then when you "know better, do better". I like to put it this way: know better (self-awareness), think better (mindset/

memories), feel better (emotionally, physically, spiritually), do better (actions), and be better (personal growth) in life and love.

Mind, Body, and Soul Approach

No matter what else you decide, be sure to focus on getting your mind, body, and soul aligned as you break habits, release negative memories and emotions so that you can be your best self.

While Western medicine serves a purpose and can be necessary during your growth and healing, during my most recent training as a school psychologist, I learned that for best results and lasting change, medication is important when necessary, but should always be coupled with two other forms of treatment for permanent lasting change. This includes things like improved eating habits (increase fruits and vegetables) and exercise or movement to increase serotonin, dopamine, and blood flow. Mental and emotional help and support is available through working with an expert or purchasing books, DVDs, or CDs to help create the mindset shifts you are looking for.

Over the years, I've found for both myself and for my clients that sometimes you may not be able to verbalize or release certain issues without mentally being walked through them to free yourself. So a beautiful coupling of what I call "East Meets West" is best. For example, prayer and meditation or exercise, coupled with teas and herbs is more effective. Simple relaxation techniques and things like Jin Shin Jyutsu, yoga or tai chi can be very powerful couples with Techniques like Emotional Freedom Release (EFT) in healing deep issues.

After surviving the fire, and overcoming everything that I shared with you in this book, I promised myself that I would laugh as hard as I could for as long as I could, when I could. And I would also make sure that I was happy, because I didn't overcome all my challenges and live to tell my story just to end up settling in Iife or spend it unhappy and unsatisfied. I wanted to figure out a way to make a difference in the lives of others on a larger scale.

I went on a journey of self-discovery and grabbed a book at the bookstore to help me find answers, get started, and discover "where to next," like you're doing now. Inspired after reading the book, I went online to see how I could put my ideas to work to help others on their journey of personal growth and development. I learned that I could make a greater impact beyond what I was already doing, but I needed to find mentors to help me along the way; and I needed to determine exactly what market or group of people to focus on serving, helping, and supporting first and for most.

Decide Where to Go Next

Whether loss of innocence stems from family issues, surviving the aftermath of a war, or any abuse committed against you, the loss of innocence leaves us roughed up and shook up emotionally and physically. Once you are able to put a name to your experience, you can then move forward with clarity, knowing why you feel the way you do.

As we lean on friends and family we trust, we can then decide what type of outside help and support we need to get unstuck, deal with the memories and emotions, the meanings we've assigned to them, and address any other roadblocks, obstacles, or challenges we face so we can live the life we want and desire.

Have you found yourself staring at the charred remains of your broken relationships, finances, or dreams? The remains of what and who you once were "before"... before you gained weight, lost money, or lost your innocence and your way?

Healing yourself and the world around you is absolutely possible as we work together to see what aspects of healing you need at this moment and time in your life today.

Taking Your Voice Global

During my work as a school counselor over the years, I often was a witness to seeing hundreds upon hundreds of sons and daughters mirror what was going on at home. This was true despite their socioeconomic status. And surprisingly, as mothers and fathers came in to meet with me, they shared how they too had struggled in high school or grew up with family problems, felt unloved, or had traumatic and dramatic experiences in their lives they hadn't received help for. That's when I decided that I wanted and needed to do more. Especially once I learned that, in most cases, there were now three generations of lost innocence taking place in one way or another.

As countless news stories came out about women being abused and staying in toxic relationships for years, it seemed that women and young girls were hurting and needed help to know they were not alone or the only ones. That's when I decided to focus on helping women: the mothers, the matriarchs of the family, aunts, sisters, cousins, nieces, friends, and next of kin. Women who had done the best they knew how, but were often suffering in silence themselves or just hadn't made the time to get support after working hard to take care of everyone else.

I also decided to focus on women who share my story of what life was like in my twenties, in young adulthood. This was a time when I was: successful by all outward appearances, but behind closed doors I was hurting inside, masking emotional pain and regret, settling for a life, career, and relationship less than what I deserved or desired.

Yes! With my mind made up, I made it my mission to help women who secretly felt powerless or unsure how to change their story, situation, or circumstances after experiencing a premature loss of innocence, and feel stuck or trapped in some way.

During that time I continued to apply the tools, tips, and suggestions in the book as I prayed and sat in silence, searching for clarity. I also signed up for my first webinar, virtual program, and workshop. At that time, I heard about "J" Delhi's daughter who was raped, tortured, and sodomized on her way home from a movie theater in India. I also heard what seemed to be story after story of women being treated like second-class citizens in their own countries or homes. And when I heard a story about a local entertainer who had committed suicide and given up on life, it broke my heart.

That's when the Personal Power Movement I created was born! Not an "us vs. them," "men vs. women" thing, but rather a movement with us all making a collective effort to achieve something great within ourselves and in turn something greater than ourselves. To be our best, do our best, give our best, and be our happiest or just plain feel good as we take care of ourselves first and then give and serve from that place.

I wanted to help and reach women around the world and on every continent, but how? One of my mentors suggested I start locally, then nationally, and go from there. I was eager, anxious, and excited as I began conducting workshops and trying to spread the word. It took several years, but then slowly but surely things began falling into place and I entered a competition to become the Next Greatest Speaker and Author. I didn't win, but I gained some valuable experience and was more determined than before as I received positive feedback from people in the U.S., Europe, and Asia.

I discovered something amazing: there was a way to take my voice global and make an even bigger and long-lasting impact. A few years later I got my online radio show and was ecstatic when I discovered that I could potentially reach millions through my show like I had hoped and dreamed.

If you feel like I do and you have it in your heart to help heal the world, then great! If you're ready to get started, you can team up with a nonprofit or community organization and volunteer, or attend a leadership training with a goal of making a lasting impact. However, before you start I want you know that as the saying goes, "Put on your oxygen mask first," meaning before you try to help save anybody else, make sure you don't over commit yourself, set boundaries, and engage in your own personal growth. You can also start healing the world locally as you create a "neighborhood watch"-type organization to keep the children safe as possible as they walk to and from school. Or like the millions of women who recently protested in the Middle East to raise awareness and promote peace, you can start to help create a shift globally. There's also the news, social media, and tons of blogs and websites that you can join or create yourself for a cultural shift right where you live.

According to UNICEF, unless the world tackles these inequities today, 167 million children will be in extreme poverty, 69 million children under age five are at risk of dying between 2016 and 2030 due to lack of health care or malnourishment, and 60 million of primary school age children will be unable to attend school. So another way to give back and become a part of a movement is to research organizations like this or one of the nonprofits I shared earlier like The Forgotten Children, Inc. and decide to give back a donation of time, attention, or financial support. Whether you decide your mission and movement is to start with creating a neighborhood watch group or be an educator in your local schools or university, or to create films, plays, and events to raise awareness, it is all meaningful, it all makes a difference and it all matters. Create a blog or join a global movement to help others overcome what you've faced. Or at the very least, which is often underestimated, is the opportunity to just be a better you and make it your mission to break the cycles and chains that have bound your family year after year, day after day.

Realize that you don't have to go it alone and that there are ladders of life, people, places, and things to support you.

Tying it All Together

We have a God-given personal power based on the simple fact that we are all human beings and we all have the same innate, inner strength to use our voice and choice. For twenty years, I have tapped into this power to help clients reclaim their innocence, save their dreams from going extinct, and restore hope to their hearts as we addressed memories, motives, decisions, and actions of the past caused by themselves or loved ones. We do this work prior to moving forward with improved coping skills and ways to courageously pursue our dreams and goals.

Now it's your turn to join the ranks of those of us who have overcome our pain and are now living our dreams. No matter who you are or what you've been through, things can and will get better. There is hope, happiness, and the life you're meant to live waiting. What else is waiting for you on the other side? Is it your heart's desire for peace, joy, love, and success? You and your dreams are worth the investment to find out. Keep going and don't give up until your pain no longer controls you. You control it and use it as fuel to ignite your passions and be your best.

Reclaiming your innocence and reclaiming your power starts one day at a time and with one action step at a time. Engage in the activities and exercises from this book to help improve your overall wellness and empower you to no longer feel the need to stay busy, overeat, overspend, overanalyze and judge others, or mask your emotional pain.

Start right from where you are, with a goal of gaining clarity and self-awareness. Gain the knowledge and understanding to discover the root cause of your issues, triggers, habits, and patterns, as well as insight on how to move forward. Uncover why you do what you do, which can be freeing and an important part of the process in learning from your past, so that history doesn't repeat itself in your life, relationships, decisions, and actions.

There are healthier, happier ways to overcome setbacks and fill any voids you're currently experiencing. Start with a decision to develop positive habits, have healthy relationships, and anything that will empower your mind, body, soul, and spirit. For example, seek spirituality in the form of mediation and prayer, and healthy physiological releases through things like yoga, tai chi, or kickboxing.

I want to encourage you and let you know that, like me, with suffering relationships, blaming yourself for everything, depressed, unable to take care of yourself emotionally, or be present for your loved ones fully.

We don't have to live in a way that looks successful by outward appearances yet we're unsatisfied in our personal lives or are putting our dreams on the shelf. Like me, you can go from feeling powerless to using your God-given talents, skills, and abilities to make an impact locally or globally, with a legacy that outlives you. The good news is that as long as we make a commitment to do our part in our immediate sphere of influence, in our lives and relationships, or with what's within our fingertips, we can also help others do the same.

In fact, I came to some realizations about the types of intimate relationships I got involved in after having my innocence stripped away sexually and being verbally and physically abused. I want to share them with you in hopes that what I discovered may help you on your journey too.

I realize that I don't have to be afraid to love and I don't have to be afraid to be alone or not chosen or wanted by someone—because I choose love, I choose me, and I want me.

I spent most of my adult life searching for and desiring love in a fear-based state, which only got me that in return (in my relationships). Rather than loving just for love's sake, just because it's fun, it feels good, or I wanted to, I entered into relationships "to be loved" rather than "be love" for the other person. The experiences I witnessed as a child had me searching for love for one of three reasons: trying to prove to a ghost of my past that I was lovable and wanted; trying to escape a life I did not want, with love as my escape route; and trying to live up to the cultural codes and expectations of the world around me.

What I did not realize was that I had been desperately seeking validation and confirmation that I was worthy of love. This resulted in me attracting men who were just as hurt if not more. And "hurt people hurt people," so this was not a good combination.

The good news is that despite all of that, I have learned the power of saying "no" and setting boundaries. They've helped me be brave enough to decide who to trust with that space; and who to invite in or out of that space as I move forward.

As you decide to take your voice global, I hope you remember that boundaries are not only spatial or physical, but there are also emotional boundaries, relationship boundaries, and communication boundaries whereby we learn to say "no". Saying "no" isn't about being mean, it's about the limits we set on how much we disclose about ourselves and our lives when we meet someone for the first time, or are still getting to know them, their heart and level of integrity.

Remembering this will help you move forward, pursue your dreams, and goals with child-like wonder and power.

Resources

Questionnaire: Answer all the questions below as best you can ... but first pause and take a nice deep breath in and out as you tell yourself, "It's time." Then complete this questionnaire.

> **Before reading this book, did you want to get better, but you didn't know how? (Please elaborate)**
>
> **In what ways is your present life being negatively affected or impacted by your past?**
>
> - Relationally
> - Financially
> - Socially
> - Emotionally
> - Personally
>
> **On a scale ranging from 0–10, with 0 being the worst your past problem or traumatic experience has impacted your life/emotions, and 10 being your past problem or traumatic experience has had no impact on your life/emotions at all, where would you rate yourself and why?**

What obstacles or challenges are you running into on your journey to growing personally? (Check all that apply)

- An unsatisfied need
- An unsolved problem
- An unachieved goal
- An unresolved pain

Do you feel stuck or torn between two parts of you (the old you vs. the current you today)? Please explain.

Do you find yourself passing down or keeping cycles going, resulting in a lost innocence continuing in your family line (intentionally or unintentionally)?

Have others moved on but you can't or it's been hard to completely move on? (Please explain why)

What would it take to increase your personal growth or your happiness this year? (Check all that apply)

- Easing emotional pain
- Addressing a need
- Solving problems
- Achieving goals
- Getting questions answered
- Other (please specify)

Don't Quit

When things go wrong, as they sometimes will
When the road you're trudging seems all uphill.
When the funds are low, and the debts are high,
And you want to smile, but you have to sigh,
When care is pressing you down a bit,
Rest if you must, but don't you quit.

Life is strange with its twists and turns, as every one of us sometimes learns, and many a failure turns about, when he might have won had he stuck it out: don't give up though the pace seems slow, you may succeed with another blow.

Success is failure turned inside out, the silver tint of the clouds of doubt, and you can never tell how close you are, it may be near when it seems so far, so stick to the fight when you're hardest hit, it's when things seem worst that you must not quit.

—Unknown author

Glossary

Adult-child experience—burdened with situations that only adults should have to address or be faced with, making adult decisions, and dealing with adult issues as a child.

Affirmations—affirming, declaring, and making a positive statement or proclamation about yourself or your situation.

Amygdala—part of the brain that plays the primary role in the processing of memory, decision-making, and emotional reactions.

Breakthrough—clarity, insight, and a new or better outlook and mindset that empowers you and helps you make shifts to take the necessary steps and actions to move forward in life.

Care plan—both things to anchor and ground you as well as things that allow the innocent child in you a chance to be care free, play, and relieve stress. This could be a fun, yet responsible play date with yourself and others. For example, swinging on swings, pajama party, trampolines, potato-sack races, hopscotch or whatever you consider fun that allows you to "just be" and take a break from what can sometimes be monotonous or mundane adult responsibilities. It could also include things like a "daycation," spa treatment, and a day of laughter.

Challenges—test or trials that show up in our lives.

Dopamine—a neurotransmitter that helps control the brain's reward and pleasure centers. It also helps regulate movement and emotional responses.

Earned security—the ability to make sense of our past experiences and problems and create new secure attachments in our current relationships with others.

Emotional Intelligence—the ability to process information and situations as they come, adapt to change, and cope in a healthy manner when faced with upsets and setbacks.

Emotional memories—emotions attached to the information and experiences that affect and impact decisions we make and the meaning and feelings we assign to those experiences.

Fight-or-flight response—our body's primary defense mechanism that occurs in our nervous system, allowing us to respond to both perceived and actual threats of danger.

Grief and loss—consciously or subconsciously grieving a loss, in this case the loss of our innocence.

Healthy connections—strong, positive relationships and connections with others that nourish us, lift us up, and are beneficial and meaningful.

Inner critic—an internal voice that criticizes us through negative words and thoughts that are often logical, but counterintuitive to our self-esteem and are usually rooted in the negative words and comments of others, masquerading as thoughts and opinions of our own.

Infographic/meme—picture with information intended to share information easily and quickly with the viewer/reader.

Innocent child—that wholesome, pure, virtuous part of us that is oblivious to danger, trusting and resilient, which allows us to be confident in ourselves and in our loved ones' ability to care for us and keep us safe.

Jin Shin Jyutsu—a self-help, self-healing technique using a disarmingly simple style of acupressure on certain points in the hands to move and shift stagnant energy.

Lost innocence—exposure to danger, witnessing or experiencing traumatizing events, and betrayals that left us with emotional or maybe even physical scars.

Mantra—an expression repeated during meditation or a positive word or expression that's repeated to serve as a trigger to get you going or to help you focus.

Mirror neurons—once thought to only exist in animals, they have now been found to exist in us and basically allow us to mimic the feelings and emotions of what we see as part of the visual-spatial part of our brain.

Memory bank—memories of our information and experiences deposited and stored in our brain.

Negative emotions—can be empowering or disempowering. For example, if used by the inner critic, our negative emotions can make us feel bad, afraid, and unwilling to try new things. However, these same negative emotions of anger, sadness, hurt, and disappointment can also be used to help us process our feelings and weigh the pros and cons prior to making a decision or taking action in a relationship or business deal. But in this case, we are referring to the negative emotions attached to past decisions and actions tied to your innocence being lost or stripped away.

Negative ripple effect—a negative ripple in your current thoughts, choices, decisions, or actions that results in relationships, circumstances, or situations that you do not want, yet keep attracting and creating in your life.

Neuropsychology—the study of the structure and function of the brain, aimed at understanding how our behavior, perceptions, and knowledge are influenced by the various parts of our brain.

Obstacles—something or someone that gets in the way or stops us from moving forward as quickly as we initially could have or would have.

Out-of-body experience—physically present, but mentally zoned out or somewhere else.

Outward appearances—the way we look or appear to others on the outside; the impression we give to others.

Personal transformation—change or a different way of thinking, seeing, and doing things.

Play therapy—a form of therapy to provide children with the opportunity to express their experiences and feelings through natural play.

Post-traumatic Grief—a condition that manifest itself on an emotional, mental, or cellular level due to neglected or unaddressed grief from the loss of someone or something we cherish and value.

Post-traumatic Stress—a disorder that develops from the negative effects of high levels of stress after being exposed, experiencing, or witnessing very traumatic or life-threatening events that shock the system.

Psychosomatic—mentally and emotionally triggered illnesses.

Roadblocks—obstacles to something we are trying to do, be, or achieve.

Safety plan—a plan to keep your positive mindset and positive energy from being stolen by negative people around you; boundaries to ensure you and your children aren't walked over or taken advantage of financially or emotionally; and/or help from experts that can help you create an "exit strategy/exit plan" for you to be able to leave an abusive relationship safely.

Serotonin—a neurotransmitter in the brain that affects emotional states and helps us feel good.

Secure attachments—parents (or guardians) make themselves physically and emotionally available as they care for and nurture us.

Self-actualization—when one reaches the highest level of their potential, talents, and personal/self-growth.

Self-awareness—knowledge and understanding to discover the root cause of your issues, triggers, habits, and patterns, as well as gain insight on how to move forward.

Self-esteem/self-worth—esteeming ourselves or seeing ourselves as worthwhile.

Self-love—loving ourselves and demonstrating so by taking care of ourselves (mind, body, and spirit, without feeling guilty for doing so).

Self-fulfilling prophecy—what we fear or dread taking place actually happens as our negative beliefs, thoughts, and actions causes it to be or makes it so.

Stages of grief—while everyone grieves in their own way and not always in the same order, most of us go through what Elisabeth Kübler-Ross described as the five stages of grief: denial, anger, bargaining, depression/sadness, and acceptance.

Steps to maturity—maturity is assumed, but does not always take place, as one grows older chronologically. Steps to maturing mentally typically occur as we mature emotionally.

The look—all hope seems lost, they're just going through the motions, their eyes are dim, there's a blank stare, or if you look deep enough, their eyes are almost lifeless. There's no emotion behind their eyes, both their eyes and body language seem to reflect lost hope, discouragement, emotional pain, and sadness.

Transition—going from one stage of development to another (i.e., from teen to adulthood).

Triggered—a situation, experience, interaction, or circumstance that set off a series of thoughts, emotions, or even memories in you that in turn affect your actions and decisions.

Unconscious mind—can be likened to an automatic pilot that goes to work and includes unfiltered thought processes, memory, affect, and motivation, whether good or bad, right or wrong, rational or irrational.

Wounded healer—someone who has emotional, psychological, mental, and/or personal wounds from life that can now be used to empathize and help heal the wounds of others with those same or similar wounds.

References

Abraham Maslow. *A Theory of Human Motivation. Psychological Review,* no 50 (1943): 370–396.

Anthony Robbins and Chloe Madanes. "Strategic Intervention." (2013) www.strategicintervention.com

Daniel Amen. Making A Good Brain Great: The Amen Clinic Program for Achieving and Sustaining Optimal Mental Performance. (Potter/Ten Speed/Harmony Books, 2006), 77–78.

Daniel Richard Miller. *The Enlightenment of Divorce: 123 Ways to be Happy Regardless of the Circumstances I've Created for Myself.* (Art of Being Productions, 2016)

Daniel Siegel. *"The Developing Mind: Toward a Neurobiology of Interpersonal Experience." (The Guilford Press, 1999), 6–45.*

Daniel Siegel and Mary Hartzell. *Parenting from the Inside Out: How a Deeper Self-Understanding Can Help You Raise Children Who Thrive. (Penguin Putnam Inc, 2003).*

Erick Erikson and Joan Erikson. *Identify and the Life Cycle* (New York: International Universities Press, 1959).

Gerald Sklsare. *Brief Counseling that Works: A Solution Focused Approach for School Counselors.* (Thousand Oaks, CA: Corwin Press, 2007).

W. Hugh Missildine. *Your Inner Child of the Past.* (Pocket Books, 1991).

John Winslade and Gerald Monk. *Narrative Counseling in Schools: Powerful and Brief.* (Thousand Oaks, CA: Corwin Press, 2007).

Robert Sepulveda. *Ladder PowerPoint.* (Verdugo Fire Academy Instructor, 2009): 7–32

Programs from L.J. Jackson:

Reclaim Innocence Classes/Programs: www.reclaimedin-nocence.com

Eliminate Stress EBook www.personalpowerwithin.com

5 Step Guide to Reduce Stress in 15 minutes or less! www. person-alpowerwithin.com

Healthy, Happy Relationships Complimentary Copy of CD Set www.personalpowerwithin.com

Wise Up and Rise Up Radio Show www.wiseupandriseupradio.com

Organizations to Support and be Supported By

American Red Cross: http://www.redcross.org/

Celebrate Recovery: www.celebraterecovery.com

Child Welfare Services: www.cahwnet.gov

California Association of Firefighters: http://www.capf.org/

Fire Family Foundation www.firefamilyfoundation.org

Forgotten Children Inc., www.forgottenchildreninc.org

GriefShare Groups: www.griefshare.org

National Domestic Violence Hotline: (800)799–7233 or (800) 799-SAFE

National Fallen Firefighters Foundation: https://www.firehero.org/

National Suicide Prevention Helpline (800) 273–8255 or (800)-273-TALK

The National Sexual Assault Hotline (800) 656–4673 or (800) 656-HOPE

Rape, Abuse and Incest National Network (RAINN): https://www.rainn.org/

Social Services Hotline: In the U.S. Call or Dial the number 211

UNICEF United States Fund https://www.unicefusa.org

World Health Organization: http://www.who.int/en/

About the Author

L.J. has years of experience working with culturally and economically diverse children, teens, and families of different nationalities. She has a passion for providing inspiration, resources, and support to help empower others and help them see beyond their current circumstances, obstacles, or "perceived limitations" to reach their desired personal and life goals.

L.J. is an inspirational speaker on the topics of reclaiming your innocence, reclaiming your personal power, becoming unstoppable despite your past, self-determination, eliminating stress, mess, and unhappiness, and eliminating fear.

L.J. is the CFO of Personal Power Within, Inc. and has a proven track record of helping thousands of people of all ages see beyond their current circumstances to "make It happen!" She was featured in *Women of Distinction* magazine and has been recognized as an Inspirational Woman of the Year by Women's Network Radio (WNRN); recognized as a VIP Professional Woman of the Year by NAPW; selected as a Woman of Outstanding Leadership by IWLA; inducted as a member into the *Continental Who's Who* of national business leaders for exceptional achievement, outstanding leadership, and professionalism; recognized as a Professional Woman of the Year by NAPW for outstanding leadership and commitment (2014/2015); and selected as a Woman of Outstanding Leadership by IWLA (2014/2015).

L.J. provides mentoring and coaching exclusively for women who are serious and ready... giving you the freedom to be real, and unmask and get to the root cause of what's keeping you from being happy, completely authentic, fully empowered, and taking action. She provides coaching and mentoring by phone and in person, speaks, and provides women's retreats. Visit www.personalpowerwithin.com and www.reclaimedinnocence.com.

Join me weekly on my Wise Up and Rise Up Radio
show, featured on the Program Your Life Radio Network
(www.wiseupandriseupradio.com).

www.Facebook.com/PersonalPowerwithLJJackson
www.personalpowerwithin.com
www.reclaimedinnocence.com

Made in the USA
Las Vegas, NV
12 November 2021

34283410R00075